PITTSBURGH STEELERS
YESTERDAY & TODAY™

ABBY MENDELSON
FOREWORD BY ANDY RUSSELL

WEST SIDE PUBLISHING

Abby Mendelson has written, edited, or ghostwritten more than two dozen books, including *The Pittsburgh Steelers: The Official History* and *Pittsburgh: A Place in Time*. The author of two novels and two short story collections, he is also the coauthor of *Pittsburgh Born, Pittsburgh Bred* (the city's official 250th anniversary book), *Pittsburgh Characters,* and *The Power of Pittsburgh*.

As a linebacker for the Steelers for 12 seasons, **Andy Russell** earned seven Pro Bowl invitations and won two Super Bowls. He went on to become a successful businessman and the head of the Andy Russell Charitable Foundation. He has also written three books: *Andy Russell: A Steeler Odyssey, An Odd Steelers Journey,* and *Beyond the Goalpost*.

Factual verification by Jake Veyhl

Special thanks to Dianne Feazell Rossini, member of the 1963 Steelerettes, who helps keep the squad's legacy alive at www.steelerettes.com.

Front cover, clockwise from left: Ben Roethlisberger, Terry Bradshaw, Franco Harris, Jerome Bettis

Back cover, from left: Art Rooney Sr., Rod Woodson, Ernie Stautner, Bill Cower

Yesterday & Today is a trademark of Publications International, Ltd.

West Side Publishing is a division of Publications International, Ltd.

Copyright © 2010 Publications International, Ltd. All rights reserved. This book may not be reproduced or quoted in whole or in part by any means whatsoever without written permission from:

Louis Weber, CEO
Publications International, Ltd.
7373 North Cicero Avenue
Lincolnwood, Illinois 60712

Permission is never granted for commercial purposes.

ISBN-13: 978-1-60553-758-0
ISBN-10: 1-60553-758-6

Manufactured in China.

8 7 6 5 4 3 2 1

Library of Congress Control Number: 2010920551

Front cover: **AP Images** (top left, top center & top right); **Getty Images** (bottom left & bottom right)

Back cover: **Corbis** Jason Cohn/Reuters (right); **Getty Images** *Sports Illustrated* (left, left center & right center)

AP Images: contents, 6, 7, 14 (top), 15, 17 (top), 18 (top), 26 (top), 27 (bottom), 28 (bottom), 30 (top left), 31 (top left), 33, 34 (bottom), 41 (bottom), 42 (bottom), 43 (right), 44 (bottom), 45 (top), 47 (top left), 48 (bottom left), 49 (top), 50 (bottom), 55 (bottom), 58 (top left), 60, 62, 63, 66 (bottom), 73 (right), 82, 83 (top), 89, 90 (top), 96, 97 (top), 98 (bottom), 99, 101, 111 (bottom), 112 (top), 114 (bottom right), 115 (top left), 116 (bottom), 117, 118 (top), 119, 120 (top), 121, 122 (right), 123 (right), 124 (bottom left), 126 (bottom), 128 (top), 129 (right), 131 (top), 132, 133, 134 (top right & bottom right); **Corbis:** 13 (bottom), 16 (right), 24, 25 (left); Bettmann, 9 (right), 21 (left center), 34 (top), 37, 38, 46 (bottom left), 72 (bottom); Matthew Cavanaugh/epa, 125 (center); Jason Cohn/Reuters, 83 (bottom); Wally McNamee, 64 (bottom), 65 (bottom); Reuters, 108 (top); Charles E. Rotkin, 23; **Frank Egan:** 42 (top); **Getty Images:** contents, endsheets, 3, 8, 19 (bottom), 26 (bottom right), 35, 57 (bottom), 59 (bottom left), 73 (left), 76 (top), 77 (top), 81, 84, 85, 87, 88 (bottom), 91, 92 (bottom right), 95, 100, 102 (top), 103 (left), 104 (top right), 109 (right), 110 (top), 112 (bottom), 113, 118 (bottom), 120 (bottom), 123 (left), 128 (bottom), 130 (top), 131 (bottom), 135 (bottom right); AFP, 50 (top), 110 (bottom), 111 (top); Focus on Sports, 39, 69 (bottom right); *Sports Illustrated,* 36 (bottom), 44 (top), 45 (bottom), 51, 54, 55 (top), 56, 64 (top left), 68, 69 (left), 71 (top right), 72 (top), 75, 76 (bottom), 79 (right center), 86, 94, 97 (bottom), 102 (bottom), 107, 122 (left), 127, 129 (left); Time Life Pictures, 9 (left), 22; **Courtesy HA.com Photography:** 10, 17 (bottom), 31 (bottom right), 46 (bottom right), 47 (bottom), 58 (bottom left), 59 (right), 70 (bottom left), 71 (top left), 79 (top), 93 (bottom right), 105 (bottom right); **D.P. McIntire:** USFL.info, 74 (bottom right); **NFL:** contents, 11, 12, 18 (bottom), 26 (bottom left), 27 (top), 40, 41 (top), 43 (left), 48 (bottom right), 52 (bottom left & bottom right), 53, 61, 65 (top), 74 (bottom left), 90 (bottom); **PIL Collection:** contents, 13 (top), 14 (bottom), 19 (top), 20, 21 (top, right center & bottom), 25 (right), 29, 30 (top right, bottom left & bottom right), 31 (top right & bottom left), 32, 36 (top), 46 (top left & top right), 47 (top center & top right), 48 (top), 49 (bottom), 52 (top), 57 (top), 58 (top right & bottom right), 59 (top left, top center & bottom center), 64 (top right), 66 (top), 67, 69 (top right), 70 (top left, top right & bottom right), 71 (bottom left & bottom right), 74 (top), 77 (bottom), 78, 79 (bottom left & bottom right), 80, 88 (top), 92 (top left, top right & bottom left), 93 (top left, top center, top right & bottom left), 98 (top), 103 (right), 104 (top left, top center & bottom), 105 (top left, top right & bottom left), 106, 108 (bottom), 114 (top left, top right & bottom left), 115 (top right, bottom left & bottom right), 116 (top), 124 (top left, top right & bottom right), 125 (top left, right & bottom), 126 (top), 130 (bottom), 134 (top left & bottom center), 135 (top left, left center & right center); **Courtesy Dianne Feazell Rossini:** 28 (top); **Shutterstock:** 109 (left); **University Archives, University Library System, University of Pittsburgh:** 16 (left)

Steelers fans take their show on the road—to Baltimore in a rivalry game against the Ravens—on November 26, 2006. In a 2008 article, ESPN.com ranked Steelers fans as the best in the NFL.

CONTENTS

Foreword 6
Loyal to the Steelers 8

Chapter One
SAME OLD STEELERS

1933–1968 10
Rooney Brings Football to Pittsburgh 12
Coping with the Depression 14
Rooney Swaps the Team 15
A Brief Taste of Success 16
The Bluefield Bullet 17
Wallowing in Mediocrity 18
Remembering Forbes Field 19
Steelers Memories 20
Steel Town 22
Ex-Lions Add Some Roar 24
Stars of the '50s and '60s 26
Steel Bad 28
Black and Gold 29
Steelers Memories 30

Chapter Two
THE STEELER DYNASTY

1969–1991 32
Noll Turns 'Em Around 34
Moving to the AFC 36
Mean Joe Greene 37
The Gunslinger 38
The Immaculate Reception 40
Drafting to the Super Bowl 42

Steelers Memories 46
"The Soul of This Team" 48
A Pair of Jacks 49
Inheriting the Throne 50
Terry's Targets 51
Corralling the Cowboys 52
The Steel Curtain 56
Steelers Memories 58
The Black Menace 60
Game Day at Three Rivers 61
Lucky XIII 62
The Last Hurrah 66
Steelers Memories 70
Secondary Terrors 72
The Turnpike Rivalry 73
The Lonely Thumb 74
Stuck in Neutral 75
Stars of the '80s 76
Steelers Memories 78

Art Rooney Sr.

The Pittsburgh Press

Terry Bradshaw

Willie Parker button and Troy Polamalu pin

Tickets to 1998 and 1995 AFC championship games

Chapter Three

COWHER POWER

1992–2000	80
The Right Man for Pittsburgh	82
Building a Contender	84
A Super Bowl Quarterback	85
Woodson Makes an Impact	86
Double Yoi!	87
To the Super Bowl, Baby!	88
Steelers Memories	92
Almost Heaven in '96, '97	94
Here Comes "The Bus"	95

World's Greatest Fans	96
Butting Heads with the Bengals	98
Blown Calls	99
They Called Him Slash	100
Rivaling with the Ravens	101
Stars of the '90s	102
Steelers Memories	104

Chapter Four

HIGH TIMES AT HEINZ FIELD

2001–2009	106
A Home of Their Own	108
Three INTs Short of a Super Bowl	110
Tommy Gun Gets It Done in 2002	111
The Go-To Guy	112
15–1 with a Rookie QB	113
Steelers Memories	114
High Five!	116
Cowher's Farewell Season	120
Tales of the Terrible Towel	121
Tomlin Takes the Reins	122
Ten Wins and a Quick Playoff Exit	123
Steelers Memories	124
Sixburgh!	126
Stars of the New Millennium	130
Falling Short in '09	132
Steelers Memories	134

Chapter Five

Steelers by the Numbers	136
Index	143

Jerome Bettis

Steelers pin

Ben Roethlisberger and the "Immaculate Redemption"

PITTSBURGH STEELERS YESTERDAY & TODAY

FOREWORD
By Andy Russell

I feel so blessed to have had the opportunity to play for the Pittsburgh Steelers—with their superb management (the Rooney family), outstanding players, and great coaches—and being a part of the enthusiastic Steeler Nation. I've been a part of the Steelers for five decades, having started my career back in 1963. Obviously it was a great thrill to survive the decade of the '60s (when we struggled to win most games) and then be one of the five pre–Chuck Noll players (with teammates Ray Mansfield, Rocky Bleier, Sam Davis, and Bobby Walden) to make it into the '70s, when the team won four Super Bowls.

Actually, in 1963 we almost won our first championship. In the final game of the regular season, we played the Giants at Yankee Stadium, a game we had to win to get into the NFL championship game against the Bears. Unfortunately, we lost that game to the Giants—a great disappointment. But I remember vividly how Mr. Rooney, despite that devastating loss, shook everyone's hand, praising our effort, wishing us good luck in the off-season, and, being the classy man that he was, caring about his players.

Steelers players, Russell included, had a lot more fan mail to open after Pittsburgh emerged as an NFL power in the mid-1970s.

One of the benefits of playing on that team (I was fortunate to start as a rookie) was having the opportunity to play with teammates who had played in the '50s—guys like future Hall of Famer Ernie Stautner, Myron Pottios, and Clendon Thomas, who taught me that the greatest badge of honor in the NFL was to "play hurt." Stautner lived up to that mantra when he continued to play with a compound fracture of the thumb. Although the bone was sticking out of the skin, he didn't come out of the game for even one play.

After spending two years in the Army (1964–65) as a lieutenant in Germany, I returned to the Steelers, who had just hired a new coach, Bill Austin. I realized that those older players had retired, as had the coach from my rookie year, Buddy Parker. Those three years under coach Austin, despite our terrible record, were important to me as I was still learning how to play the game. It was also amazing how supportive our fans were even though we were losing.

On a USO tour during the 1968 Tet Offensive in Vietnam, I visited a hospital full of our badly wounded soldiers. Trying to comfort them, I was stunned when one of the injured yelled, "Go, Steelers!" Back home, it was also impressive to observe how the Rooneys refused to panic. They supported their players and coaches, always patting us on the shoulder and encouraging us.

Then in 1969, the team hired Chuck Noll, who truly was a genius and a great man to work for. Coach Noll's first speech was right to the point, as he informed us that the reason we had been losing is that we weren't focused enough on the details. He was convinced that "success is in the details," and we memorized the opponents' tendencies in great detail!

Despite coach Noll's brilliance, we would post a record of 1–13—yes, 13 straight losses. But Coach never lost us, always

FOREWORD

In the first six years of the 1970s, Russell made the Pro Bowl each season.

speaking the truth, saying, "We are going to get worse before we get better—because I'm going to require you to play the game with proper techniques, no gimmicky stunts to help us get by."

One of his key decisions in 1969 was to draft Joe Greene, truly the NFL's player of the decade. Over the next six years, the team would put together awesome drafts, selecting such future Hall of Famers as Terry Bradshaw, Jack Ham, Franco Harris, Lynn Swann, John Stallworth, Jack Lambert, Mel Blount, and Mike Webster.

In 1972, Franco Harris began moving the sticks on third and mid-long (normally a passing down). He had an amazing year, beating Oakland with his sensational "Immaculate Reception," considered the greatest play in NFL history. We would lose to the Miami Dolphins in the AFC championship game, but we were on the right track.

We had a good year in 1973 (10–4) but lost to a very good Oakland Raiders team, as we had just not figured out how to make the big plays at the right time to get ourselves into a Super Bowl. But in 1974, in another AFC championship game, Jack Ham made the all-time most important play in Steelers history when he intercepted Kenny Stabler late in the game to get us into our first Super Bowl, No. IX. We went on to beat the Vikings to get our first ring.

One year later, we found ourselves in Super Bowl X against a very good Dallas Cowboys team. By playing our strong defense, and with Terry Bradshaw connecting with Lynn Swann on hugely athletic receptions, we went on to beat the Cowboys and win our second straight Super Bowl.

During those Super Bowl years, Steelers center Ray Mansfield and I went around the world five years in a row, visiting such places as Tokyo, Seoul, Hong Kong, Bangkok, Singapore, New Delhi, Saudi Arabia, Kuwait, Frankfurt, and London. We gave speeches, participated in football clinics, signed autographs, gave interviews, and went on radio and TV shows. Little did we know at the time that we were meeting some of the foreigners who would become part of the Global Steeler Nation in future decades.

In my last year, 1976, we tried to make it three in a row. Unfortunately, the Steelers did not make it to the Super Bowl for two years (it's hard to repeat), but they did win another two in a row for four out of six years.

In the 1980s and '90s, the Steelers had many good players but often came up just short of getting into the Super Bowl. When they made it to the Super Bowl in the 1995 season, they lost to the Cowboys. Coach Bill Cowher finally put together the kind of players he wanted—Jerome Bettis, Ben Roethlisberger, and Hines Ward—and the Steelers won their fifth Super Bowl in February 2006. People joked that the Steelers had "won one for the thumb," but that ring was all theirs—their first. Now with coach Mike Tomlin, the Steelers are the only team in the NFL to have won six Super Bowls.

The stories and photographs in this book conjure up some of my fondest memories. I hope you will enjoy this nostalgic look back at one of the greatest teams in sports history, the Pittsburgh Steelers.

Andy Russell

Andy Russell

PITTSBURGH STEELERS YESTERDAY & TODAY

Loyal to the Steelers

The story of the Pittsburgh Steelers is about far more than football. It's about hard work and loyalty. About a town that lost and found itself. About a love so profound that it exceeds words—and passeth understanding.

The story begins with a town on the western frontier. Beginning life some 250 years ago, Pittsburgh was a river town, a trading post, the place where explorers Lewis and Clark set off for parts unknown. Then came coal and oil and steel, the black of the earth, the gold of gain. Virtually overnight, the city of Pittsburgh began to dominate the industrial world—arming the nation, building the Panama Canal, erecting the Empire State Building.

Through all the successes emerged an attitude. Labor was paramount; company success came before self. Pittsburghers did their jobs and didn't brag. They didn't preen or parade or pout. They just did it—clean and hard and honest.

In time, steel moved elsewhere. The black, mammoth mills shut down, and corporations skulked away. For a moment, it seemed there was nothing left.

Except a football team.

In 1933, Art Rooney, a big-time horseplayer and small-time sports promoter, bought a franchise in the new National Football League. At the time, selling sports didn't seem like a good bet. In the depths of the Depression, when people barely had enough money for footwear much less football, Rooney stubbornly stayed at the helm. As times changed, and his team appreciated in value, Rooney was too loyal to the town to take the big-money offers to move the team away.

Still, the Steelers lost . . . and they lost and they lost—for 40 years. Through it all, the Rooneys never complained. They never blamed the town or the fans for anything. Instead, their players laced up their cleats and tightened their chinstraps and hit the line.

Loyalty is a hallmark of Steelers football. In the notoriously fickle world of professional sports, the Steelers have, over the last 40 years, had only three head coaches. Patient with their own people, the Steelers have reached the postseason some two dozen times and won a record six Super Bowls. Through it all, the team has been true to Pittsburgh's core values—low-key, personal and professional, relying more on pile-driver hits than flashy plays or fancy talk.

But there's more than unprecedented football success that accounts for the nation's premier fans. As difficult as it is for outsiders to understand, or believe, the people of Pittsburgh love their city—its powerful history, rugged beauty, ethos of hard work. Ex-patriots or not, Pittsburghers love these hills, these valleys.

In January 2006, when the Steelers needed to win three playoff road games to reach the Super Bowl, fans recalled team founder Art Rooney, who had never lost faith in his team. This fan keeps the faith at Invesco Field in Denver during the AFC title game.

INTRODUCTION

Lunch-bucket tough, blue-collar strong, Pittsburgh's Depression-era steelworkers were the perfect touchstone for the city's new NFL team.

"Whether you're a stockbroker or 7–11 clerk," explained fan Amy Michalic, "you're equal in the Steeler Nation. There's a commonality that allows you to take part without fear of discrimination. It truly brings Pittsburghers together."

On Game Day in Pittsburgh, both blue- and white-collar workers paint their faces black and gold. Babies from West Mifflin to Mt. Lebanon keep clean with their Steeler bibs.

"Isn't it exciting?" asks Dr. Audrey Guskey, a Duquesne University marketing professor. "It's given us such life and energy, unified the whole community—all demographic groups. The great thing is, it wasn't created by marketers. It comes from the heart of the people. *We're* dreaming it."

That dream began on the North Side of Pittsburgh a very long time ago.

Mobbed by fans at Three Rivers Stadium minutes after his 1972 Immaculate Reception, Franco Harris celebrates the miraculous catch that beat the Oakland Raiders 13–7 and gave the Steelers their first postseason win in 40 years of existence.

By the 21st century, there was so much accumulated pride in this team and this town, which had been battered so long by economics, that Pittsburgh was ready for a renaissance of its own. A people's renaissance. A rebirth of recognition—of everything they love about this city. They found it in something they could unabashedly cheer: their football team.

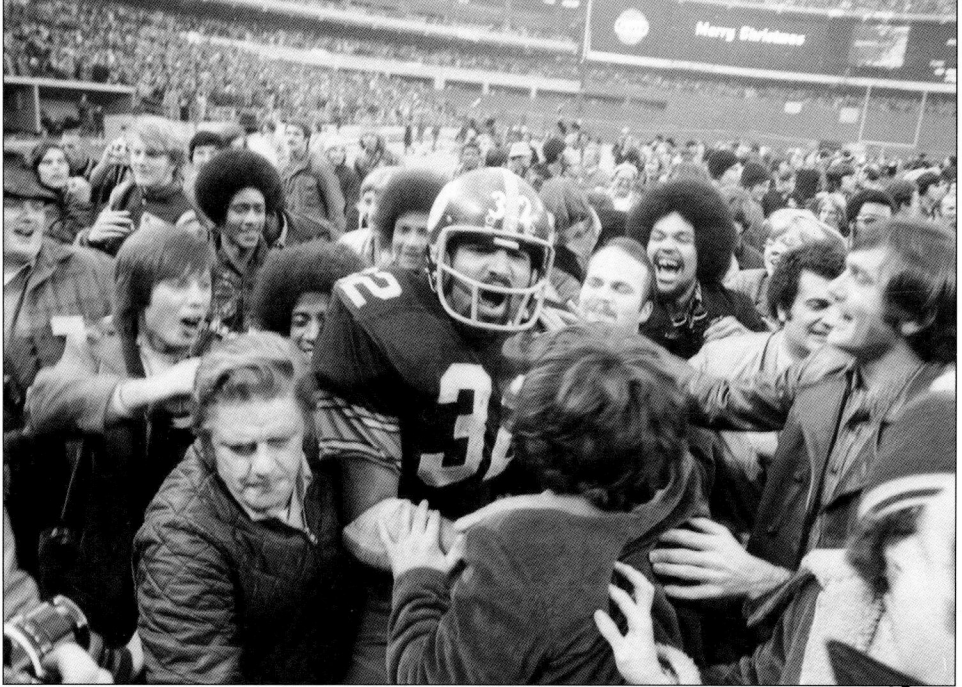

CHAPTER ONE

SAME OLD STEELERS
1933–1968

"Forty years of losers, and he hated to lose."

—Art Rooney Jr., summing up his father's first four decades as Steelers owner

Above: *Prior to the switch to Darth Vader-esque black in 1963, the Steelers' helmets were white and gold. As today, they featured the Steelmark logo, a symbol of the steel industry.* **Right:** *Deep into their long era of incompetence, the Steelers faced the Rams at the Los Angeles Coliseum on December 12, 1948. On their way to an embarrassing 31–14 loss, the inept Steelers defense trailed the play. Empty seats attest to Pittsburgh's anemic drawing power.*

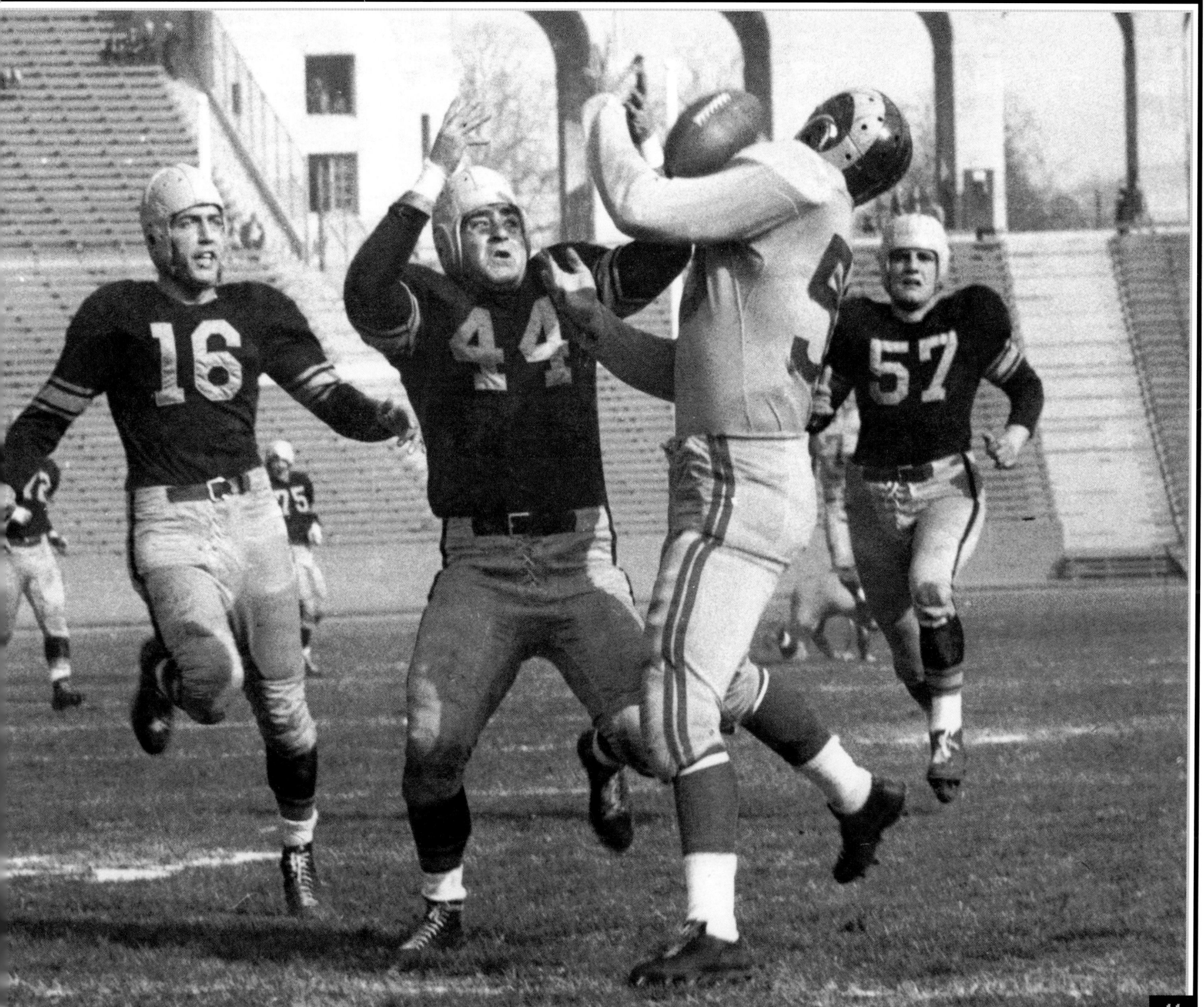

Rooney Brings Football to Pittsburgh

He was looking for a little cachet, Art Rooney was, so he bought into a newfangled thing called the National Football League.

It wasn't necessarily a great idea, especially in Depression-era Pittsburgh, where mills were closed and Apple Marys stood on every corner. But Rooney's friends, George Halas of the Chicago Bears and Tim Mara of the New York Giants, waved him aboard, and he went.

All of 32 years old in 1933, Rooney was no stranger to the sports world. After growing up on Pittsburgh's tough North Side, where he lived above his father's saloon, he became a champion amateur boxer, a minor-league baseball player, a football player, and a prizefighter good enough to consider boxing his way around the world.

Rooney, who was known for his dapper suits and big stogies, was also a card player, horseplayer, and boxing promoter—big enough in his time to stage championship bouts. Intensely devoted to his family and his town, Rooney eschewed the road to stay home.

Despite Pennsylvania's restrictive Blue Laws, Sundays were devoted to football (at least after church). Rooney, who had promoted various sandlot and semipro teams, got the chance to transform his rough-and-tumble Majestics into the NFL's Pittsburgh Pirates (who would be renamed the Steelers in 1940). Rooney plopped down $2,500 and went for it.

"My father loved the game," said his son Art Rooney Jr. "And he loved the relationships, the environment, the players, the camaraderie with the other owners. That was a labor of love. But football also gave him credibility. He wasn't just a guy who bet the horses; he owned the Steelers."

Playing in cavernous Forbes Field, whose grass was muddy in the fall and frozen in December, Rooney ran the team out of a hotel office (where the card game never seemed to end). His "files" were a pocket notebook held together with rubber bands. While he may have rubbed shoulders with royalty, Rooney never lost contact with the street—or his own bare-knuckled past. One time, he and coach Luby DiMelio were discussing where athletes tended to stay in better shape, in the ring or on the gridiron. When coach DiMelio didn't quite get the point, the "Chief"—a nickname his sons gave him, taken from the *Adventures of Superman* TV series—moved the desks, put on boxing gloves, and proceeded to clean the coach's clock.

Fisticuffs aside, Rooney became the most beloved person in Pittsburgh history because he invariably treated others with dignity and respect. "His real thing was dealing with people," said his son Dan Rooney. "He made you feel as if the most important thing he had to do was to talk to you. He made you

Art Rooney gained instant cachet in 1933 when he upgraded his semipro Majestics into an NFL franchise, the Pittsburgh Pirates (who were renamed the Steelers in 1940). He would own the team for 55 years.

> "HE MADE YOU FEEL AS IF THE MOST IMPORTANT THING HE HAD TO DO WAS TO TALK TO YOU. HE MADE YOU FEEL AS IF YOU WERE A FRIEND. IT WASN'T PLANNED, AND IT WASN'T CALCULATED."
>
> —DAN ROONEY, ON HIS FATHER

SAME OLD STEELERS: 1933–1968

In Depression-era Pittsburgh, the Pirates were NFL doormats, going 22–55–3 from 1933 to '39. They played to thousands of empty seats in cavernous Forbes Field, home of the major-league baseball team of the same name.

feel as if you were a friend. It wasn't planned, and it wasn't calculated."

If that went for civilians, it was doubly true for his players. He made a point to learn all their names. Knowing himself what it was like to play, Rooney never berated his players. Instead, he offered encouragement. Often, even after losing seasons, players would find themselves the recipients of unexpected bonuses.

Said Art Rooney Jr.: "My father always told us, 'Treat everybody the way you'd like to be treated. Give them the benefit of the doubt. But never let anyone mistake kindness for weakness.' He took the Golden Rule and put a little bit of the North Side into it."

"I always looked on him as a special person," said Joe Greene, a mainstay of the 1970s Steelers dynasty. "That was the edge we had as a football team. We did it for the Chief."

On November 15, 1938, Byron "Whizzer" White carries the ball during an exhibition game against the independent Los Angeles Bulldogs.

A Good Day at the Track

It was actually two good days at two tracks. Two legendary days in 1936—made all the more so by the myth that surrounds them.

"My father," Art Rooney Jr. remembered, "was the best horse handicapper in the world."

A gamblin' man with an eye for horseflesh and a mind to calculate the odds, Rooney went to two New York State racetracks—Empire City and Saratoga. Accounts of his day differ. Some say he began with $300 and ran it up to $21,000 at Empire City, then moved over to Saratoga. By the time he was finished, Rooney had won as many as 11 races in a row and walked away with at least a quarter-million dollars.

Others claim the Chief won $380,000; some say more. Whatever the figure, he stuffed his winnings into a rented armored truck, returned home, and told his wife, Kathleen, that they'd never have to worry about money again.

Coping with the Depression

During the 1930s, the Pirates remained solvent despite never finishing with a winning season. Their 6–6 season in 1936 was their best effort. For the decade, they were 22–55–3.

"When my father started the club," Art Rooney Jr. pointed out, "everybody was on the breadline. The genius was to keep the [team] in business—not to win or lose, but to stay in business. The logical way was to do that by winning, but that wasn't always the truth. You stayed in business by keeping your payroll in shape."

Winning? "He hated to lose," Rooney continued. "He was the greatest horseplayer of his time, and he knew how to win. And he was no fool in the business of football. But the big thing was to survive."

Rooney signed college grads and cronies. His first-ever No. 1 draft choice, Notre Dame's William Shakespeare, never bothered to play. Those who did play got a C-note per game for their pains; i.e., bruised muscles and busted noses. That was good money when workingmen's wages were $40 per week.

That was more than enough money to attract John McNally, also from Notre Dame. The only problem was that, in 1934, McNally was still enrolled at the Catholic university. In fact, he even played for the Fighting Irish that year.

In the bad old days, Pittsburgh had enough good starting players—from Johnny Blood to Bill Dudley—to stay competitive. The problems arose when the first-stringers were injured and the team had to play the scrubs, who couldn't compete.

The Whizzer

Whenever the Chief found a legitimate gate attraction, he'd sign him. Witness his first big score: Byron "Whizzer" White.

An All-American at the University of Colorado, White was the NFL's first big-money player—great on the field, Gibraltar-solid at the box office. Playing tailback in a single-wing offense, and hating his nickname, White led the league in 1938 in both rushing and salary. He racked up 567 yards while earning $15,000—triple what the NFL's best were getting. The Whizzer scored four of the team's ten touchdowns that year as the Pirates went 2–9.

White left after the 1938 season to take a Rhodes scholarship at Oxford University. He entered the field of law, and in 1962 he was appointed by President John F. Kennedy to the U.S. Supreme Court, where he served for 31 years.

Byron White

No problem! On Saturdays, he was demur collegian John McNally. On Sundays, he was dashing Johnny Blood, the name from Rudolph Valentino's *Blood and Sand*.

In a decade of forgettable players, Hall of Famer Johnny Blood was Pittsburgh's first true star. A bantamweight halfback, he left Rooney's team after 1934 and then returned for three more years, as a player (1937–38) and a coach (1937–39). In 1937, Blood led the club with 10 receptions, good for 168 yards and 4 touchdowns.

Though a terrific player, Blood was a world-class carouser and a crummy coach. In his three seasons behind the bench, he won only six games.

Same Old Steelers: 1933–1968

Rooney Swaps the Team

In the fall of 1940, as war raged across Europe, the Steelers were on the verge of extinction. At a time when NFL franchises were folding or relocating, the Steelers limped through a 2–7–2 season in 1940 while Art Rooney struggled to balance the books.

To make matters worse, Rooney had agreed to help out a personal friend and cross-state rival, Eagles owner Bert Bell, who was having his own financial troubles.

So, in a celebrated three-way sale-swap, the Steelers were officially sold to New York financier Alexis "Lex" Thompson for $160,000. Thompson was to move the Steelers to Boston, where he planned to call them the Iron Men, while Bert Bell's Eagles, tentatively called the Keystoners, were to divide their time between Pittsburgh and Philadelphia. "To this day," said Dan Rooney in his book *My 75 Years with the Steelers and the NFL*, "the complexity of this crazy deal makes my head spin."

Needless to say, the idea of the Steelers leaving Pittsburgh sent shockwaves through the community. "Don't worry, Danny," the Chief assured his tearful son, as recalled in Dan's book, "we're not going to sell the team. This is just something we have to work out."

But before it was over, the deal was blocked. Other NFL owners, it turned out, did not want Rooney to control the entire state. The peace was quickly made when the Steelers' players moved to Philadelphia as Thompson's new Iron Men, while Bert Bell's old Eagles came to Pittsburgh—as the Steelers. Bell came, too, to coach and take a 50-percent share in the club.

On the plus side, the Steelers finally got some firepower, including Penn State's Chuck Cherundolo, who would stay 20 years as a player and coach. Unlike patrician Whizzer White, Cherundolo was the club's first working-class hero. A rugged, square-jawed plugger from Wilkes-Barre, Cherundolo starred at center and linebacker.

With Bell as the coach in 1941, the Steelers started playing midcentury ball. They employed the new man-in-motion T-formation, which the Chicago Bears had used so successfully. Unfortunately, that system didn't work in Pittsburgh. With the team in shambles early in the 1941 season, Rooney replaced Bell with Duquesne University football coach Buff Donelli, whom Rooney in turn had to fire because he rarely came down from the Bluff (Duquesne's campus). The Chief replaced him with Walt Kiesling.

All told, the 1941 Steelers ended the season with three coaches, one victory, and America at war.

> "Don't worry, Danny, we're not going to sell the team. This is just something we have to work out."
>
> —Art Rooney, to his young son

Helmetless New York Giants kicker Ward Cuff nails a 23-yard field goal against Pittsburgh on October 20, 1940, at the Polo Grounds. New York waltzed over the Same Old Steelers, 12–0, in front of 19,000 sleepy fans.

A Brief Taste of Success

With the exception of signing Whizzer White, bringing Jock Sutherland back to town was Art Rooney's greatest public relations coup.

It was 1946, and Rooney hired legendary University of Pittsburgh player and coach John Bain Sutherland to lead the club. As an All-America lineman for Pop Warner's Pitt Panthers, Sutherland had starred on national championship teams in 1915 and '16. After graduation and a dentistry degree, Sutherland was coaching his alma mater by 1924. Over the next 15 seasons, through 1938, he racked up 111 wins—more than any coach in Pitt history. He went undefeated four times, taking the national title in 1937.

Adding both science and sense to the Steelers, Sutherland not only turned the Steelers around, but also swelled the team's coffers, filling cavernous Forbes Field. As part of the new breed of NFL coaches, Sutherland used playbooks, game films, classroom sessions, detailed scouting reports, and even a sideline chalkboard for diagramming plays. Jock Sutherland was everything his predecessors weren't—a man with a system and a vision.

In 1946, Pittsburgh finished with a respectable 5–5–1 record. The next season, the Steelers went 8–4 and tied the Eagles for first place—the team's best finish until the 1970s. Injuries dashed their hopes, however, as the Steelers lost the playoff to Philadelphia 21–0.

The 1946 hiring of Jock Sutherland, the University of Pittsburgh's winningest coach, became the Steelers' first good attempt to bring stability to the team. Although his Steelers tied for first place in 1947, his 1948 death sent the club into a 20-year tailspin.

Justifiably, fans had high hopes for 1948, but that spring Sutherland died suddenly of a brain tumor. "He gave Pittsburgh fans the kind of teams they were looking for," Art Rooney recalled. "If it hadn't been for the Doctor, I never would have been able to continue in pro football."

The Steagles and Card-Pitt

To field an NFL team, an owner needs able-bodied football players. That seems simple enough, but it wasn't during World War II, when the able-bodied were fighting across the globe. That left defense workers and 4-F rejects to man NFL squads.

To fill out their teams, the owners came up with a novel idea. In 1943, when the Steelers numbered just six players and the Eagles roughly double that, they merged. "Had to do it," Steelers co-owner Bert Bell told *The New York Times*. "Pittsburgh had no backs left and Philadelphia had no linemen."

Washington Redskins versus Card-Pitt (light helmets), October 29, 1944

Officially called the Phil-Pitt Eagles, they were known as the Steagles. The following year, 1944, the Steelers merged with the Chicago Cardinals, becoming Card-Pitt. Although the team names are memorable, the quality of play was forgettable. The Steagles went 5–4–1, and Card-Pitt was the league's doormat in 1944, finishing with an 0–10 record.

SAME OLD STEELERS: 1933–1968

The Bluefield Bullet

For as many drafts as the team blew in its first decade—they traded draft pick Sid Luckman to the Bears, for example—every so often the Steelers got things right. In the first round in 1942, they took Bill "Bluefield Bullet" Dudley, a 172-pound halfback, future college and pro Hall of Famer, and the club's brightest star over its first 20 years.

Virginia's first All-America player, Dudley certainly didn't look the part. Undersized and underweight, Dudley "did everything wrong," said Dan Rooney. "He couldn't throw. He was not fast. He was not big. He couldn't kick. But he led the league in ground gained and interceptions. He was one of those players. Dudley was intelligent and explosive. He was a winner."

No doubt about that. As soon as the 1942 season began, Dudley proved his mettle, running the season-opening kickoff back to the Eagles' 35. Then, two plays later, he raced in for a touchdown. The following week, Dudley returned the Redskins' second-half kickoff for a score. Although the Steelers lost those games, they finished the campaign with a 7–4 record—their first winning season. The Bluefield Bullet's 696 rushing yards paced the NFL, and his 6 touchdowns and 438 passing yards led the squad.

After losing two years to the war, Dudley returned in 1945 to lead the team in scoring, but the Steelers stumbled to a 2–8 finish. Then came a new coach, the revered Jock Sutherland. On paper, the Doctor-Bullet combo seemed like sheer dynamite. It wasn't.

Predictably, Sutherland wanted the game played by the book. "This is the way things are going to be," the exasperated Sutherland told his recalcitrant star. "No deviations."

But Dudley, being Dudley, deviated—to great advantage. In 1946, the Bullet led the Steelers in scoring while topping the NFL in both rushing (604 yards) and interceptions (10, a team record that stood for nearly 30 years). It was good enough to net him the NFL MVP Award.

Unfortunately, it wasn't good enough for the Doctor, who didn't like Dudley's wide-open style and was unsatisfied with the team's 5–5–1 record. Feeling he had enough talent without his maverick halfback, Sutherland traded Dudley to the Detroit Lions.

Too bad, because when the team came up short in the playoff game against the Eagles, they could have used the Bluefield Bullet.

A first-round draft pick in 1942, halfback Bill Dudley did it all—ran, threw, intercepted, and kicked. Dudley led the Steelers to their first winning season (1942), served in the military for two years, and then returned as a team leader in 1945 and '46.

> "HE COULDN'T THROW. HE WAS NOT FAST. HE WAS NOT BIG. HE COULDN'T KICK. BUT HE LED THE LEAGUE IN GROUND GAINED AND INTERCEPTIONS. HE WAS ONE OF THOSE PLAYERS."
>
> —DAN ROONEY, ON BILL DUDLEY

A fan favorite, Bill Dudley signed this miniature helmet later in life. He was 89 when the Steelers won their sixth Super Bowl in February 2009.

PITTSBURGH STEELERS YESTERDAY & TODAY

Wallowing in Mediocrity

Following the sudden death of Steelers head coach Jock Sutherland in April 1948, it seemed sensible to elevate his aide-de-camp as coach. Although he was a decent man and a credible assistant, John Michelosen was just the wrong guy to coach the Steelers. Following his mentor to a fault—and not keeping up with a game that was changing dramatically in the postwar years—Michelosen couldn't get the team above .500. While insisting on using Sutherland's antiquated single-wing formation, Michelosen went 20–26–2 in his four years as Pittsburgh's head coach (1948–51).

From 1948 to '56, the Steelers seemed to slide through slush. Sometimes, though, players such as Jim Finks, Elbie Nickel, and Jack Butler were enough, as at snow-covered Griffith Stadium (pictured) on December 16, 1951. The Steelers took the Redskins 20–10.

Two head coaches followed Michelosen from 1952 to '56, Joe Bach and Walt Kiesling, but the results were predictably mediocre. Bach went 5–7 and 6–6, while Kiesling sandwiched two 5–7 seasons around a 4–8.

"We had some good ballplayers," recalled cornerback Jack Butler, who holds the Steelers record with four interceptions in a single game. "We could play games. We could win games. But we didn't have enough."

Sure, the Steelers had memorable players. In 1952, for example, quarterback Jim Finks threw for 2,037 yards and a league-leading 20 touchdowns, and Elbie Nickel ran for 884 yards. Then there was defensive tackle Ernie Stautner, whose patented 18-wheel hits were fan favorites. A rock-solid 230 pounds, Stautner was the last Steelers star to play both ways. But it was on defense that he shined. In one game, he sacked the Giants quarterback on three straight plays.

Unfortunately, Butler and Stautner weren't enough. "The thing the Steelers lacked was depth," Dan Rooney recalled. "When they got hurt—and you get hurt in this game—it would be a disastrous blow."

Steeler fans yearned for a championship-level coach. In late August 1957, just days before the start of the season, Art Rooney finally found his man.

Who Needs Johnny U?

Unitas as a Steelers rookie in 1955

Johnny Unitas is the all-time greatest Steeler who never played for Pittsburgh.

Born and raised in the Steel City, Unitas was undersized and injured at the University of Louisville. He hung around in the 1955 NFL Draft until the Steelers picked him with the 102nd pick.

At training camp, Unitas impressed Dan Rooney and his brothers—and no one else. With coach Walt Kiesling favoring Jim Finks at quarterback—and Vic Eaton and Ted Marchibroda behind Finks—there was no room on the roster for Johnny U. Kiesling cut him.

Signed by the Colts, Unitas became one of the greatest players in NFL history, winning NFL championships in 1958 and '59 and Super Bowl V in 1970.

Besides Unitas, western Pennsylvania has produced more than 40 NFL quarterbacks, including Pro Football Hall of Famers George Blanda, Jim Kelly, Dan Marino, Joe Montana, and Joe Namath—all of whom played elsewhere.

SAME OLD STEELERS: 1933–1968

Remembering Forbes Field

It was a time before Steeler gear and the ubiquitous Terrible Towel. It was a time when crowds were dominated by men, and adults dressed like adults, not players or children. It was a time before luxury boxes and in-seat wait service and valet parking.

It was Forbes Field.

One of baseball's first concrete and steel ballparks, Forbes Field opened as the home of the National League's Pittsburgh Pirates in 1909. The stadium sat varying numbers of people over the years, but generally hovered around 35,000 (which the Steelers rarely needed). Set at the edge of verdant Schenley Park, in the Oakland section of Pittsburgh, it was a glorious green space in summer—and muddy, ugly, and iced over by December.

It was where the Steelers played for 30 years, 1933 to 1963.

This cold, unlovely place was so dangerous that, in 1944, leading rusher Johnny Grigas quit the team rather than run on the ice. "No honor is worth the risk," he wrote to Art Rooney.

Perhaps the top Forbes Field moment came on snowy November 30, 1952, when the team whipped the Giants 63–7. After Lynn Chandnois ran back the kickoff, and Jim Finks threw for 254 yards and 4 touchdowns, the 15,140 fans tore down the goalposts. It was a Steelers first. For the record, the largest crowd for a Steelers game at Forbes was 40,916 (standing room only) on September 30, 1962. The weather was decent, and the Giants were in town.

Finally, on December 1, 1963, an era ended. It was none too soon, longtime ticket baron Joe Carr would tell you. Carr remembered the days when 2,000 souls rattling around Forbes Field was a big gate. Still, others had fond memories of the cold, barren stadium. "The place was ours," recalled longtime fan Joe Chiodo. "We sat anywhere we wanted."

Forbes Field housed Pittsburgh's NFL team from 1933 to '63. Frequently muddy, usually cold, and often bereft of fans, it was a working-class ballpark—but only for those who could bear to see the Black and Gold lose regularly.

On November 20, 1954, fans at Forbes Field saw their mediocre team (5–7 in 1954) line up against San Francisco—and lose 31–3. The rare appearance by the talented 49ers meant an unusual sellout for Pittsburgh.

When Pitt Stadium Was Home

Unlike Forbes Field, Pitt Stadium was a real football home.

The University of Pittsburgh opened this classic, unsheltered bowl in 1925 to accommodate the huge crowds who watched championship-level college football. Seating nearly 70,000, it was the perfect home for the Panthers.

Not so for the Steelers, who toiled to half-empty houses. After playing some games at Pitt Stadium after the university acquired Forbes Field in 1958, the Steelers played there exclusively from 1964 to '69.

The greatest Pitt Stadium moment came on September 20, 1964, when *Pittsburgh Post-Gazette* photographer Morris Berman captured Giants quarterback Y. A. Tittle kneeling in the end zone, helmet off, exhausted, bleeding. The photo made *Life* magazine and became an iconic image of old-time NFL football.

Finally, in 1970, the Steelers moved to a new, modern facility, Three Rivers Stadium, their home for the next 31 seasons.

STEELERS MEMORIES

Led by coach Walt Kiesling, the Steelers enjoyed their first winning season in 1942, going 7-4. On November 29, the date of this program, the Steelers shut out the soon-to-be-defunct Brooklyn Dodgers 13-0.

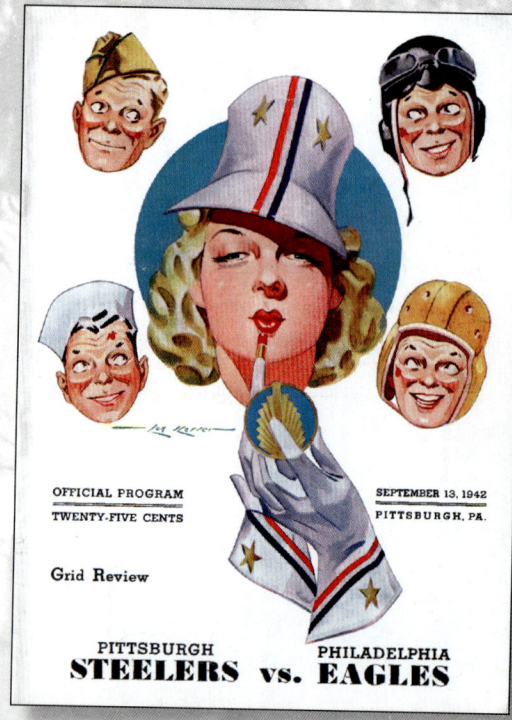

Begun as a workingman's blue-collar attraction, the Steelers by the 1950s had become family fare. Inexplicably, this doll has the characteristics of the fairer sex.

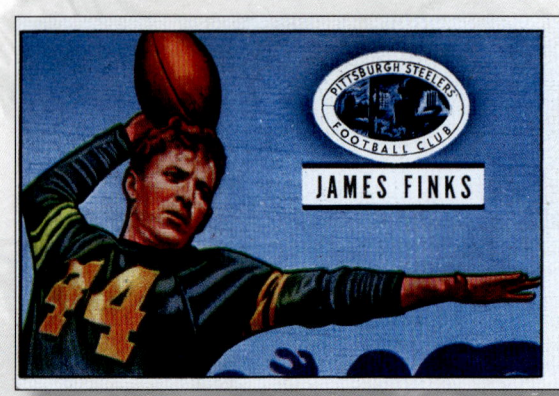

Steelers quarterback Jim Finks earned All-Pro honors in 1952 and led the NFL with 2,270 passing yards in '55. Finks earned induction into the Pro Football Hall of Fame as an executive after helping transform the Vikings, Bears, and Saints into winners.

In 1942, as this program indicates, the Eagles and the Steelers adopted military themes. A year later, as World War II deepened, both teams were so weak that they merged, forming the Steagles.

Go Steelers

From the beginning, fans collected Steelers gear, such as this bench warmer for those damp, chilly days at Forbes Field and Pitt Stadium. Fans could sit on the bench warmer or raise it up like a banner.

As plastic helmets were introduced in the 1950s, teams experimented with different face guards. Here, Steelers Russ Craft, Jim Finks, Jim Brandt, Jon Schweder, Elbie Nickel, Bob Gaona, and Dale Dodrill model various designs.

Old-timers may recall the Steelers' exciting 4–1 start in 1955, which included a 13–7 victory over the Eagles. Unfortunately, Pittsburgh lost its last seven games.

During the tenure of single-wing throwback coach John Michelosen (1948–51), the Steelers posted a 20-26-2 record. Against the Eagles in 1950, as this program uncannily predicted, the Eagles came out on top, 17–10.

Steel Town

Pittsburgh in the 1950s was a tough and brawny town. With its hard weather and rugged landscape, the city proudly bore the scars of its history, such as the Whiskey Rebellion and bloody railroad and steel strikes. During the Homestead Strike of 1892, union men opened fire on Pinkerton agents, who were heading upriver to reopen Mr. Frick's mills.

Pittsburghers loved that fight—over the steel that built the world. Over the coal that fired its furnaces.

A century ago, and less, Pittsburghers worked in mills and mines and railroads. It was hard physical labor—hot, dirty, dangerous. Pittsburghers knew that they had to be tough to live here, to survive, to succeed. Pittsburgh wasn't a place for the gentle-hearted.

By 1945, the famous black skies had cleared. Smoke Control dictated that scrubbers take the soot from the air—soot that covered everything, that made men wear two shirts a day. By the 1950s, the smoke may have dissipated, but there were still air inversions and hot, sulfur-filled nights, when it seemed that everybody's bedroom was ten feet from the Number Two Stack, when seemingly every vista showed a mill burning in the night. A century before, *Atlantic* writer James Parton famously described Pittsburgh as "hell with the lid off."

The 1950s were the heyday of Big Steel, but also of urban redevelopment, when impatient, imperious, long-visioned, and short-tempered David Lawrence reigned as the most popular mayor in Pittsburgh history. Impeccably dressed, and known for banging his large ring to signal that meetings were over, Lawrence was elected a record four times—and remade the city.

Serving from 1946 to '59, Lawrence forged a partnership with the corporate community to redevelop Pittsburgh. His extraordinary changes included transforming more than a quarter of downtown through such projects as Point State Park, Gateway Center, Mellon Square, and Mellon Arena.

In 1955, that kind of change—Pittsburgh shrugging off its dirty, industrial past to become a shimmering corporate center—drew veteran *Life* photographer W. Eugene Smith. What began as a simple three-week photo assignment to shoot

At Irvin Steel, life was hot, hard, and heavy. Pittsburghers knew that this was the world's steel capital, and they knew the dangers involved and how resilient steelworkers had to be. They expected the same from their football team.

A structural steelworker stands proud in 1956. After World War II, Pittsburgh reveled in its renaissance, which transformed a smoky, dirty city into the Golden Triangle. Similarly, the Steelers—once perennial losers—rose to NFL dominance in the 1970s.

SAME OLD STEELERS: 1933–1968

100 photos morphed into a two-year, 17,000-image obsession. By the end, Smith's book *Dream Street* had redefined Pittsburgh. It was viewed as a city of heavy industry and natural beauty, smokestacks and church spires.

Pittsburgh football reflected the city. It is not now, nor ever was, a product of elite schools, of the Ivy League, of *boola boola* and old Eli Yale. Hardly.

> "... HELL WITH THE LID OFF."
>
> —*ATLANTIC* WRITER JAMES PARTON, DESCRIBING PITTSBURGH

In 1955, Pittsburgh's football players—be it those in high school, semipro leagues, or the NFL—were mill hands and the sons of immigrants. Many of them had never learned English, but they learned enough to do their jobs. They didn't whine. They didn't complain. If things got tough, they tightened their chinstraps, adjusted their helmets, and hunkered down.

For Pittsburghers, sports became their mirror, their great equalizer, their way out of the mills and the mines. The harder they played—the harder they hit—the better. There was no other way; there was no retreat, no surrender.

When Texas was largely cattle ranches and wide-open spaces, Friday Night Lights was Pittsburgh—and Pittsburgh fans. For the hardcore, nothing symbolized the city so much as the Steelers, who were born a hard-hitting team. Cut from a pattern of dark wool, muddy boots, work gloves, and whipcord trousers, Pittsburgh fans braved any weather for a game.

This was a silent, surly time, when a cocktail shaker meant a pint of cheap rye whiskey. Football, especially Steelers football, was an all-male preserve, a proving ground, a rite of passage. There were no fancy banners or window dressings. No costumes or face painting. Players wore jerseys; fans wore pea coats that they brought home from hitches in the Navy.

Players and fans were tough guys, ready to turn the joint into a punch palace, ready for a rough-and-tumble Sunday afternoon. On Monday, the players nursed their bruises while the fans hitched up their work pants, hoisted their lunch buckets, and pulled another shift.

"Winning was not a concern of ours," said old-time Steelers fan Joe Chiodo. "It was how hard they played. Jack Butler, Ernie Stautner... those incredible defensive hits made your week."

The former Jones and Laughlin steel mill stood on the Monongahela River just west of downtown Pittsburgh. The mills' blue-collar ethic—bring your lunch bucket, don't showboat, don't complain—transferred to the Steel City's football team.

PITTSBURGH STEELERS YESTERDAY & TODAY

Ex-Lions Add Some Roar

On paper, it wasn't such a bad idea: Part company with retread coach Walt Kiesling and bring in Buddy Parker, a proven winner. Let him reshape the team in his image, bringing to the Steel City the style and smarts with which he had so much success in the Motor City.

It is true that Parker won his share of Steelers games—more than any other coach in Steelers history up to that time. But in terms of building a championship team, he was first cousin to a disaster.

Like many NFL coaches of his time, Parker preferred to fill his squad with veterans. After all, experienced players didn't make mistakes. That philosophy had worked well in Detroit, where Parker's Lions had roared their way to two NFL championships. "Parker," Dan Rooney said, "was a very able coach."

In 1958, the Steelers traded with Detroit for three-time NFL champion quarterback—and world-class carouser—Bobby Layne. Quarterbacking the Steelers from 1958 to '62, the future Hall of Famer led the team to three winning seasons—but no championships.

Arriving in August 1957, Parker felt he had to establish himself as boss, so he cut popular and successful running back Lynn Chandnois. (Soon afterward, Parker watched game films of Chandnois and witnessed his considerable skills. "If I'd had known that," he admitted, "I never would have let him go.")

The following year, Parker traded for Bobby Layne, his championship field general with Detroit. A legend on the field and off, Layne was a hard-living, hard-drinking, go-for-broke quarterback.

> "WE NEVER HAD ANYBODY LIKE BOBBY LAYNE.... HE PLAYED ONE WAY—ALL OUT."
>
> —STEELERS CORNERBACK JACK BUTLER

Dan Rooney remembered picking up Layne at the airport and driving him to practice, then held at Pittsburgh's South Park. On the way, Layne peppered Rooney with questions about the team, and when they arrived Layne immediately got down to business. "When he went on the field," Rooney recalled, "Bobby Layne was in charge. *In charge.* There was no question from the first minute."

Layne, who had led Detroit to titles in 1952, '53, and '57, gave Pittsburgh its most potent offense since the days of Johnny Blood—and commanded immediate respect. With Layne at the helm in 1958, the previously hapless Black and Gold went 7–4–1. "We never had anybody like Bobby Layne," cornerback Jack Butler recalled. "He was 100 percent competitive. He was a smart ballplayer. Win at all costs. There was no in-between, no gray area. He played one way—all out."

Wrote Dan Rooney in his autobiography: "I remember once we played the Giants and he threw only 10 passes the whole game, but three of them were for touchdowns. He could run the ball, too. He was smart—one of the smartest quarterbacks we ever had—and he did whatever it took to win."

Same Old Steelers: 1933–1968

The Steelers of the early 1960s had talented players, including (left to right) Preston Carpenter, Buddy Dial, and John Burrell. Unfortunately, they played for Buddy Parker (far right). Though he had been a winner in Detroit, in Pittsburgh Parker's anger and arbitrary cuts created more fright than fight.

Parker later admitted that dumping Layne was a mistake.

As if the cuts weren't bad enough, the Steelers were light on young talent. In two years—1959 and '63—Pittsburgh didn't select a player until the eighth round. In 1961, Dick Hoak was chosen in the seventh round—as the team's second pick.

Finally, with Dan Rooney assuming a greater role in club affairs, he demanded less panic and more planning. After the 1964 season, in which the Steelers stumbled to a 5–9 record, Parker was gone. His eight-season total: 51–48–6.

Although the team colors were black and gold, the Steelers also stood for red, white, and blue. As a patriotic gesture, the team sponsored Armed Forces benefit games (exhibitions), including this 16th version with the Chicago Bears on September 8, 1961.

On dirt infields, including the one at Forbes Field, Layne dropped to one knee in the huddle and drew up plays in the dirt like a schoolboy.

In 1962, Layne's Steelers finished 9–5 and in second place in the East Division—good enough for a berth in the Playoff Bowl. But the subsequent 17–10 loss to Detroit enraged Parker, and he forced Layne to retire.

Just as Jock Sutherland had discovered 16 years earlier when he cut halfback Bill Dudley, Parker realized in 1963 that he could have used a good field marshal in the last game against the Giants, which Pittsburgh needed to win to earn a spot in the NFL championship game. As with Chandnois,

The 1962 Playoff Bowl

It was an idea whose time was mercifully brief: have a postseason bowl game to establish bragging rights for—third place!

Variously called the Playoff Bowl, the Bert Bell Benefit Bowl, and other epithets (some unprintable), the NFL sponsored it for ten years, 1960 to '69, at Miami's Orange Bowl. In 1962, the Steelers played in the game for the first and only time, facing Buddy Parker's and Bobby Layne's old team, the Detroit Lions.

Fueled by a 9–5 season, the Steelers went steaming into the postseason looking for respectability. After all, with a team boasting three future Hall of Famers in Layne, John Henry Johnson, and Ernie Stautner, it was time for the Steelers to step up.

Playing before 36,284 fans on January 6, 1963, Pittsburgh's Dick Hoak ran in a touchdown and quarterbacks Ed Brown and Layne threw for 150 yards. But the Lions logged six sacks, picked off two passes, and blocked a field goal. The final: Detroit 17, Pittsburgh 10.

The game was ultimately forgettable, but it did result in one memorable change. The Steelers wore their black helmets that day for the very first time.

Stars of the '50s and '60s

No, the Steelers teams of the 1950s and '60s were never great. But on any given Sunday, the hard-hitting Black and Gold were capable of beating the best.

The reason, in part, was because the Steelers always had good players. Running back **Lynn Chandnois** (1950–56), for example, was capable of busting off good runs at any time. In 1952, he returned two kickoffs for touchdowns and averaged a league-best 35.2 yards per return.

End **Elbie Nickel** (1947–57), a powerful blocker, notched more then 5,000 receiving yards. Tackle **Frank Varrichione** (1955–60) went to five Pro Bowls, and **Pat Brady** (1952–54) led NFL punters with a booming 46.9 average in 1953. Guard **Dale Dodrill** (1951–59) was a four-time Pro Bowler, and back **Fran Rogel** (1950–61) rushed for 3,271 yards as a Steeler. Tight end **Buddy Dial** (1959–63) racked up more than 4,700 yards receiving.

Equipped with good moves and better hands, three-time All-Pro tight end Buddy Dial was a top Steelers receiver. He totaled more than 4,700 receiving yards in his five years in Pittsburgh before being traded to the Cowboys following the 1963 season.

The first Steeler to have his number retired, Hall of Fame defensive tackle Ernie Stautner (1950–63) is remembered for the crushing hits that took him to nine Pro Bowls. Despite broken ribs, shoulders, hands, and nose, Stautner missed only six games in his career.

Two players stood out as superstars: corner **Jack Butler** (1951–59), who picked off 52 passes and was named to five Pro Bowls as a Steeler, and defensive tackle **Ernie Stautner** (1950–63). "He was 100 percent football player," Butler remembered. "He was strong, relentless, and never gave up. He loved the game and played it to the hilt."

Under coach Buddy Parker, the Steelers fleshed out the roster with veteran stars—champions in other cities—who added both power and panache to the Black and Gold. Defensive tackle **Eugene "Big Daddy" Lipscomb** (1961–62) played only two seasons in Pittsburgh after earning All-Pro honors and winning an NFL championship with the Baltimore Colts. Tipping the scales at 295 pounds—enormous for that era—Lipscomb was a classic impact player and a fan favorite.

His counterpart on offense was **John Henry Johnson** (1960–65), part of Parker's championship dynasty in Detroit. A classic power back, Johnson rushed for 1,000 yards twice with the Steelers. "He was a great football player," Jack Butler

Acquired from Detroit in 1960, John Henry Johnson became Pittsburgh's first great power running back. As a Steeler from 1960 to '65, the future Hall of Famer ran for two 1,000-yard seasons (1962 and '64), becoming the first in team history to reach that mark.

gushed. "He could do everything. He was tough. He was strong. He could run. He could block. He could catch. He did it all."

Another Parker trade brought long-term dividends. Acquired from Philadelphia in 1964, center **Ray Mansfield** played and played and played—182 consecutive games (1964–76). "I always worked hard," he said. "I hustled. I ran downfield. I was strong and quick. My attitude always was, 'Never say die. Never be defeated. Go down fighting on the beach.'"

It didn't hurt that Mansfield was a student of the game, as were two long-term standouts who played in the 1960s. Running back **Dick Hoak** came from Penn State in 1961 and stayed for 45 years. He lasted 10 years as a player and 35 more as a coach. "I didn't have all the talent in the world," Hoak said. "I had to get every edge that I could. I had to study the game. I had to know what everyone else was doing on the field. I knew what the quarterback was supposed to do. I knew what the defense was supposed to do."

Then there was linebacker **Andy Russell**, selected in the 16th round in 1963. After losing two years to the Army, and playing from 1966 to '76, Russell "really wanted to be successful," he said. "Since I lacked certain physical talents—strength, size, and speed—I had to make up for it some other way." So he studied, took game films home—anything to give him an edge. "I prided myself in being able to know the opponents," he said. "I knew what they were going to do before they did."

> "MY ATTITUDE ALWAYS WAS, 'NEVER SAY DIE. NEVER BE DEFEATED. GO DOWN FIGHTING ON THE BEACH.'"
> —STEELERS CENTER RAY MANSFIELD

Hardworking linebacker Andy Russell went from 16th-round draft pick to play in seven Pro Bowls. Russell displayed uncanny smarts and tenacity during his 12 years in Pittsburgh.

Groundbreakers

Although the first Pittsburgh Pirates NFL team, in 1933, was integrated by former Duquesne lineman Ray Kemp, the Pirates/Steelers remained all white for the next 19 years. "You didn't have an abundance of black guys playing in the white universities that the NFL recruited," explained African American Bill Nunn, who joined the Steelers as a scout in 1967. "Black players played in black schools, and the pros didn't scout there."

Dan Rooney remembered that it was a struggle to get black players into the league. In 1952, for example, the Steelers drafted Jack Spinks, a running back from Alcorn A&M. Rooney recalled: "One man said, 'We can't have Spinks. He doesn't even have a coat.' My Uncle Jim said, 'He can have my coat,' and took his coat off and gave it to Spinks."

African American Lowell Perry joined the Steelers in 1956, but he played just six games as a receiver and kick returner before suffering a career-ending injury. Art Rooney, who visited Perry every day in the hospital, promised him a job when he recovered. In 1957, the Chief made Perry the Steelers' receivers coach—and the first black coach in NFL history. In 1966, he became the first black TV football analyst for CBS.

Lowell Perry

Steel Bad

How bad were the Steelers of the mid-1960s? Bad enough that center Ray Mansfield, who came in a 1964 trade with the Eagles, didn't want to report to Pittsburgh. "It was the joke of the National Football League," he recalled. "The team was so pitifully out of shape. The theory was that you played yourself into shape. But we were so out of shape, we couldn't play."

In 1964, head coach Buddy Parker and his Steelers self-destructed. The veterans were getting old, and Parker's cuts and disposal of draft choices had decimated the team. After a 5–9 season in '64 and the Steelers in free fall, Parker had to go.

In 1965, the Rooneys chose their new head coach, Mike Nixon, who had served as a Steelers assistant under Parker as well as under Jock Sutherland in the 1940s. Left with little talent and with no plan to improve, Nixon went 2–12 in 1965 and was gone after the season.

Next up was Bill Austin, a former Vince Lombardi assistant who came with a gilt-edged recommendation. But Austin was the worst type of disciplinarian. He berated players publicly and did not enforce his own rules. "It was crazy," Andy Russell remembered. Dan Rooney recalled that as a head coach, Austin was in over his head.

Austin so overworked his players in practices that some suffered serious injuries, includ-

Steelers safety Clendon Thomas, wearing the infamous batman jersey, watches as New York Giant Aaron Thomas snags a Fran Tarkenton pass in a 28–20 win on November 19, 1967. Mediocre on both sides of the ball, Pittsburgh finished at 4–9–1.

The Steelerettes

Pittsburgh's Steelerettes were nothing like the Dallas Cowboys Cheerleaders. When they hoisted their megaphones at Forbes Field and Pitt Stadium from 1961 to '69, they wore full, pleated skirts, long sleeves, and caps. These college women were selected on the basis of appearance, personality, coordination, gymnastic ability, and academics. They were required to maintain a 2.0 GPA—and even pass a written test.

Although popular, the Steelerettes did not make the 1970 transition to Three Rivers Stadium. Their look was outdated, prompting suggestions that they dress in more revealing costumes. That idea did *not* sit well with the straight-laced Art Rooney. "Let 'em go to burlesque," he growled.

The Steelers never had cheerleaders again.

ing career-wrecking knee injuries and dangerous concussions. After Austin's team finished 2–11–1 in 1968, for a three-year record of 11–28–3, Dan Rooney had had enough.

"Austin had lost the team," Ronney recalled in his book, "and I knew I had to make a change. I could see the fallacy in how we were doing things. I was trying to bring the Steelers into the modern era, and I knew that the right coach was the key."

SAME OLD STEELERS: 1933–1968

Black and Gold

Pittsburgh is known for black and gold. They are the colors of MLB's Pirates, the NHL's Penguins, and, of course, the Pittsburgh Steelers. This striking color scheme dates back 250 years, to Sir William Pitt, whose crest included the signature colors plus blue and white.

Roughly a century after Pitt, civic leaders began using black and gold as emblems of Pittsburgh—black for iron and coal, gold for the money they made. Eventually the colors were adopted for the city crest—and in 1925 the short-lived NHL Pirates made them the team colors. When Art Rooney's semipro football squad rolled into the NFL in 1933, he took not only the city colors but added the city seal to the jersey.

The city-seal jerseys didn't last long, but the color scheme remained the same. In 1948, the baseball Pirates followed suit. In 1980, the Penguins completed the triumvirate, making Pittsburgh the nation's only city to have all of its professional sports teams wear its civic colors.

Getting back to the Steelers, they remained staunchly black and gold—and logo-less—until 1962, when a Republic Steel representative showed the Steelmark symbol to Dan Rooney. Developed in 1958 by U.S. Steel, and adopted as a symbol by the entire industry, it included three geometrical figures called astroids, all within a circle. Representing the lightness, smartness, and versatility of steel, it immediately appealed to Dan Rooney, who thought about putting it on the players' gold helmets in place of their numbers. Not certain if they'd like it, Rooney told equipment manager Jack Hart to put it on the right side only.

Then, as if the new logo had willed it, the team rolled to the best season in its history in 1962, going 9–4 and earning a spot in the Playoff Bowl. To celebrate, the Steelers changed the helmet to black to better display the new logo.

Hart asked if he should put the logo on both sides of the black helmet.

"We got here with the logo only on the right side," Rooney answered, as recalled in his autobiography, "so let's keep it that way."

But the Steelers lost that game, and 1962 is a long time ago, so why not have it on both sides now? Rooney stated that it was a curiosity, which was a good enough reason not to change it.

One thing the Steelers did change was the jerseys. In 1966, they adopted a V-shaped gold neckline, which resembled Adam West's Batman outfit on the popular TV show. Outfitted like caped crusaders, the Steelers were losers again—and looked silly doing it. The team unveiled a new uniform in 1968, and have stuck with that basic design ever since.

Since their first season, the Steelers have worn black and gold—except during World War II when they donned green and white. As seen in this collectible montage, the designs have changed many times, beginning with the city-seal jerseys in 1933 and the jailhouse-stripes look in 1934.

STEELERS MEMORIES

Keep that wrist steady! Quarterback Jim Finks shows two Sisters of Mercy nuns how to chuck the pigskin at a Steelers training camp at St. Bonaventure College in Olean, New York, in 1955.

In 1952, Pittsburgh brought back Joe Bach, who had coached the team in 1936. Against the Eagles, previewed in this program, the Steelers played just well enough to lose, 26–21.

Halfback Dick Hoak was just 23 years old when the Steelers honored him with a tribute day in 1963. An article in this program noted that Hoak soothed "a coach's occupational ulcer" with his consistent play.

Iron City, Pittsburgh's oldest brewery, produced many commemorative Steelers cans. Pictured is center Ray Mansfield, one of several Steelers to play for both Buddy Parker and Chuck Noll.

After Steelers linebacker Mike Henry (1959–61) was traded to Los Angeles, he shed his jersey for a leopard-skin loincloth. Henry, posing here with co-star Sharon Tate and a tame lion in 1965, played Tarzan in three films.

On October 4, 1959, the Steelers had more rushing yards, passing yards, and first downs than Washington. Of course, the Redskins won the game, 23–17. Pittsburgh finished at 6-5-1 that season.

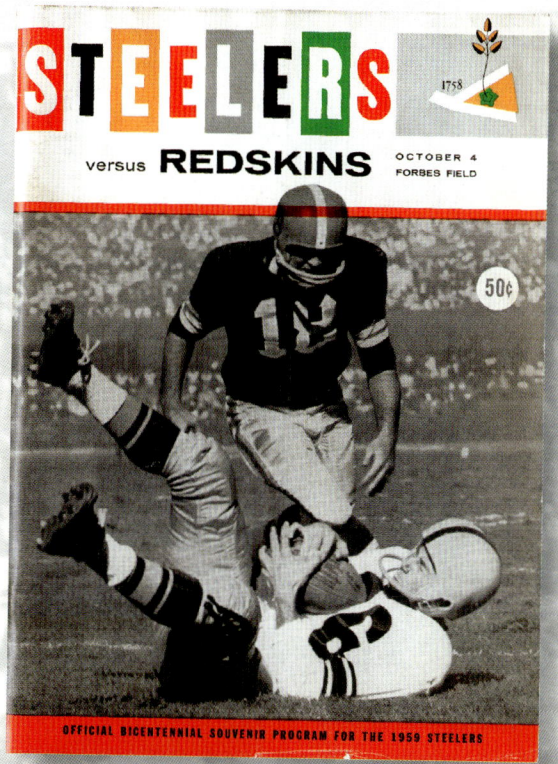

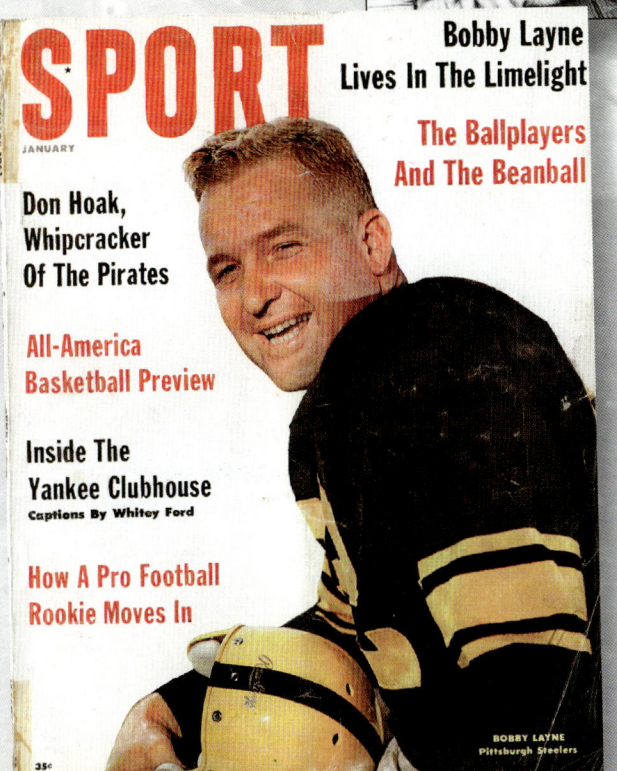

Pittsburgh's first great field general, quarterback Bobby Layne was known to diagram plays in the dirt of the gridiron. In January 1961, he made the cover of Sport magazine.

Steelers Hall of Famers Mel Blount and Ernie Stautner signed this helmet. The son of a Bavarian coalminer, Stautner weighed 230 pounds and delivered 1,000-pound hits.

CHAPTER TWO

THE STEELER DYNASTY
1969–1991

"Our goal is to win the Super Bowl."

—Rookie head coach Chuck Noll in his first team meeting, 1969

Above: *When Chuck Noll came to the Steelers in 1969 for his first head coaching job, his pledge to the perennial losers was to win a championship. Within a mere six years, he succeeded—with three more coming.* **Right:** *Terry Bradshaw hands off to Rocky Bleier in Super Bowl XIII, the Steelers' third Super Bowl victory and second over the Cowboys.*

Noll Turns 'Em Around

Funny, nobody laughed at Chuck Noll, the former Baltimore Colts assistant, when he told a perennially losing team that it was headed for the Super Bowl. After all, Noll came to the Steelers in 1969 with sterling credentials; he had played for legendary coach Paul Brown in Cleveland and had shared the sidelines with coaching genius Don Shula in Baltimore. Vince Lombardi himself had touted Noll as the next great NFL coach.

There was something about this 37-year-old's steely determination, his obvious intelligence, that commanded respect from his players. Noll began to inspire hope in veterans such as Ray Mansfield and Andy Russell, who cared about football and hated to lose.

"He was an extremely impressive guy," Russell remembered. "Very bright."

That's what the Rooneys saw, too. After Super Bowl III, which Noll's Colts had just lost, he sat for two hours with Art Sr. and Dan Rooney, discussing the Steelers in great depth and with remarkable familiarity. After the meeting, the Chief told Dan, "Don't let Noll's name get off the list."

A serious student of the game, Chuck Noll learned his football from Paul Brown and honed his skills as an assistant coach in San Diego and Baltimore. His long hours in the film room contributed to eight consecutive division titles.

Dan didn't need convincing. "Noll was the guy," he recalled. "His knowledge of the game and his intelligence were excellent. So was his commitment."

Dick Hoak, then a Steelers running back and later a Noll assistant, saw it right away. "You could tell there was a difference," he said. "Chuck knew what he wanted to do. He knew the type of players he wanted. He wanted to build through the draft. He wanted guys who understood the game. He had a plan. You could see it."

While laughs were few and far between with coach Noll, the wins weren't. The future Hall of Famer, pictured just after the Immaculate Reception, went 193–148–1 as Steelers coach, winning more games than all previous Steelers coaches combined.

That plan never changed, even though the 1969 season was a train wreck, with the new coach going 1–13. "We were pathetic," Mansfield said. "But Chuck never lost his cool. He went right back to his plan."

"Having been on championship teams," Noll said, "I had a pretty good idea of what I wanted."

That, more than anything else, cemented him as coach in the minds of the franchise owners. "You know when I knew we had a coach?" the Chief said to the assistants late one night. "When we won one game and lost 13 but he never lost the team."

For 23 seasons, 1969 to '91, Noll never lost his team. The Steelers enjoyed 13 consecutive nonlosing seasons, 1972 to '84, including the glory years when Noll became the first NFL coach ever to win four Super Bowls. He won each of his Lombardi Trophies over a six-season span, 1974 to '79.

Noll accomplished it all without tirades or temper tantrums. "People think motivation is yelling at somebody," Noll said. "It's not. It's [teaching players] *how* to do something. Because if you know how to do something, you *want* to do it because you're successful at it. Success breeds wanting to do more and to have more success."

"You prepare hard," Noll added, "and you expect to be successful. To play well, you have to have that state of mind."

The Steelers had it in abundance.

> "HE WANTED TO BUILD THROUGH THE DRAFT. HE WANTED GUYS WHO UNDERSTOOD THE GAME. HE HAD A PLAN. YOU COULD SEE IT."
>
> —STEELERS RUNNING BACK DICK HOAK, ON CHUCK NOLL

Stern, steely, and smart, Chuck Noll brought determination, discipline, and focus to the Steelers. The gritty look on Terry Bradshaw's face reflected the team's will to win on December 29, 1974, when they defeated Oakland 24–13 in the AFC championship game.

The Super Scout

Although the 1960s Steelers weren't all white, the team did not take advantage of the great wealth of African American football talent. By the late '60s, that situation changed due to the pioneering efforts of newspaperman-turned-scout Bill Nunn Jr.

A star basketball player in his younger days, Nunn became the sports editor of the *Pittsburgh Courier,* a highly respected African American newspaper. At a time when the mainstream press ignored athletes at small black colleges, Nunn covered them in depth. He also covered what he called the Black College Game of the Week, and each year he presented the Black College All-America Team.

Bill Nunn Jr.

In 1967, Dan Rooney approached Nunn to scout for the club. Later, when Nunn was elevated to front-office duties, he became the NFL's first African American club official.

Nunn's finds included John Stallworth, Mel Blount, Ernie Holmes, and Donnie Shell—all major contributors to the 1970s Steelers dynasty. "They didn't get any recognition anywhere other than the black press," Nunn said. "There's no doubt that it gave us an edge."

"Chuck didn't have to give pep talks," Terry Bradshaw said. "He drafted people who were self-starters—people who couldn't stand to lose."

"Some people say Chuck was lucky," Mike Wagner said, "but I don't think so. I think he was able to do three things: bring talent, put it together in a package, and let everybody play football. And it worked. It absolutely worked."

"We could have gotten by without some players," Jack Ham added. "But we couldn't win championships without Chuck Noll… He was able to make players *believe* that we had a championship football team."

PITTSBURGH STEELERS YESTERDAY & TODAY

Moving to the AFC

There's no war like a civil war, and no fight like a family fight. So it was in the world of pro football.

It all began when Lamar Hunt tried to buy an NFL franchise. Spurned, he began his own rival football league in 1960. As had occurred in baseball some 60 years prior, the new American Football League began to bid high for top talent—including super prospect Joe Namath, who signed with the AFL's New York Jets in 1965.

The new AFL not only carved out lucrative territories in Denver, Houston, Buffalo, and Dallas, but also went head-to-head with their older rivals in New York and the Bay Area. The truce was uneasy but bloodless—until the NFL's New York Giants raided the Buffalo Bills' roster. That's when the two commissioners, the NFL's Pete Rozelle and the AFL's Al Davis, agreed to peace talks.

By June 1966, the rivals had agreed to merge. By 1967, the leagues were using a common draft, thereby ending the bidding war. In 1970, there would be one league—the NFL—with two conferences, AFC and NFC.

Since the new NFL would be lopsided—there were 10 AFL teams and 16 NFL teams—they agreed to move three NFL teams to the new AFC. But which three?

Of course, no NFL team wanted to move. In the days before automatic sellouts, why give up traditional rivalries? To sweeten the deal, Rozelle decreed that each moving team would receive a $3 million bonus, the monies paid by the other NFL teams. The AFL wanted the Steelers, Baltimore Colts, and Cleveland Browns—three traditional NFL teams that would give the new AFC cachet.

Predictably, Dan Rooney bristled at the idea. Why should the Steelers move? What about their fans—and such traditional rivalries as Washington, Philadelphia, and New York? But in the end, money talked. That $3 million was a pretty good payday for essentially doing nothing.

Not wanting to go alone into the new arrangement, the Rooneys discussed the move with Browns owner Art Modell. Finding common cause, Modell and the Rooneys agreed to come over—if they could stay in the same AFC division. *Done,* answered a triumphant Rozelle, who stocked the AFC Central with the Steelers and Browns from the NFL and the Cincinnati Bengals and Houston Oilers from the AFL.

And with that, a new era began.

As the NFL grew and realigned, the Steelers accepted a move to the American Football Conference. Beginning in 1970, the Black and Gold had new foes, including the Buffalo Bills.

Steelers running back Preston Pearson carries the ball in Pittsburgh's first-ever game against the Miami Dolphins, on November 14, 1971. The following season, Miami would defeat the Steelers in the AFC championship game during their fabled undefeated campaign.

THE STEELER DYNASTY: 1969–1991

Mean Joe Greene

The Steelers' meteoric rise to greatness began with not only Chuck Noll but also with his 1969 No. 1 draft pick, future Hall of Famer Joe Greene.

No other player so epitomized the transformation of the franchise, its desire to win, and its willingness to do anything to succeed as Joe Greene.

Born Charles Edward Greene, "Mean Joe"—a nickname he picked up in college and always despised—played at little-known North Texas State. Normally, coming from such a school would have caused Greene to be overlooked in the NFL Draft. But Noll, as a Baltimore Colts assistant, had scouted Greene and had witnessed his strength, ferocity, and leadership. "He never lost a battle," Noll remembered.

Standing 6'4" and weighing 275 pounds, Greene played 181 games at left defensive tackle for the Steelers from 1969 until his retirement in 1981.

"Joe Greene was unrelenting," Steelers linebacker Andy Russell recalled. "He made huge plays when they had to be made. He was just an awesome addition to our squad. He hated to lose; he hated to get beat. And he refused to accept that we were losers. He was unquestionably the Player of the Decade [in the NFL]. There was no player more valuable to his team."

Setting the tone for the Steelers dynasty, Greene demanded all-out effort from his teammates—and gave the same himself. Boss of the clubhouse, commander of the defense, he instilled more fear into his teammates than the coaches did.

One time, Greene banished fellow lineman Ernie "Fats" Holmes from the field for freelancing. When defensive coordinator George Perles screamed at Holmes to go back into the game, Fats refused. "Not until Joe says I can," the 300-pound Holmes said sheepishly.

"He was like a beacon," Noll remembered. "He set a different standard from the people we had at the time."

"He was the best leader I've ever seen," Dan Rooney added.

Greene was virtually unblockable. "When he decided to come," former trainer Ralph Berlin said, "it did not matter. People had never seen anything like Joe Greene." He proved that time and again. Like the time he won a playoff game by sacking Houston quarterback Dan Pastorini five times.

The NFL's Defensive Rookie of the Year in 1969, Greene also took Defensive Player of the Year honors in 1972 and '74. He amassed 66 sacks and 16 fumble recoveries in his career, and he played in 10 Pro Bowls, 6 AFC title games, and 4 victorious Super Bowls.

"Losing," he said, "was not something I tolerated. Coming to Pittsburgh, I didn't want to tolerate it. It was as simple as that."

When he was coming, nothing could stop him. The Steelers' No. 1 pick in 1969, Charles Edward "Mean Joe" Greene demanded all-out play from every Steeler on the field. In 1994, he was selected to the NFL 75th Anniversary All-Time Team.

> "HE WAS UNQUESTIONABLY THE PLAYER OF THE DECADE. THERE WAS NO PLAYER MORE VALUABLE TO HIS TEAM."
>
> —STEELERS LINEBACKER ANDY RUSSELL, ON TEAMMATE JOE GREENE

The Gunslinger

It was 1970, a new decade, a new home in Three Rivers Stadium, and a young coach in Chuck Noll—who had gone 1–13 with the Same Old Steelers the previous year. The upside was that the team had the No. 1 overall pick in the 1970 NFL Draft. To no one's surprise, the Steelers selected quarterback Terry Bradshaw out of Louisiana Tech.

Gifted with great on-field presence, natural leadership ability, and a rifle arm (in high school, he had set a national record in the javelin with a chuck of 245 feet), Bradshaw seemed to be the quarterback the team needed to win. The reaction at training camp was immediate. "Terry Bradshaw had more talent at his position than anybody I'd ever seen," said Dick Hoak, whose last year as a player was Bradshaw's first season.

But as Bradshaw and his supporters quickly learned, there's a world of difference between the college game and the pros. "Terry was not a surprise," Noll recalled. "Terry's ability was to throw long. But it takes more than the quarterback. If you don't have people around you, you're not going to function very well."

So in 1970 and '71, the team continued to flounder, going 5–9 and 6–8. "I didn't learn any football in college," Bradshaw admitted. "I didn't learn anything about coverages. So I had this whole big adjustment."

That wasn't the half of it. Bradshaw had to contend with two other young, hot shot quarterbacks. Local hero Terry Hanratty (drafted by Pittsburgh in 1969) had made the cover of *Time* and *Sports Illustrated* while playing for Notre Dame, and "Jefferson Street" Joe Gilliam (taken in the 1972 draft) was a flashy long-thrower from Tennessee. But Hanratty was hurt and uninspiring, and Gilliam, while brilliant, was erratic.

It was up to Bradshaw to lead the team—and Noll to put him in position to do so.

"He was as good a football player as I've ever seen in my life," Dan Rooney declared, "and he may have been Noll's best effort. Chuck handled Bradshaw perfectly. He'd give him sympathy. He'd be tough. He'd talk to him and tell him what to do. He let Bradshaw call the plays. Chuck really did the job."

Said Bradshaw: "Chuck recognized my strengths—strong arm, impatient, hated short passes, loved to challenge safeties and corners as opposed to linebackers—and put this offense in for me. The thing I learned early is that you put a defense

> "CHUCK RECOGNIZED MY STRENGTHS— STRONG ARM, IMPATIENT, HATED SHORT PASSES, LOVED TO CHALLENGE SAFETIES AND CORNERS...."
>
> —TERRY BRADSHAW

Though his hands were the same size as Bradshaw's, President Richard Nixon—a former bench-warmer for Whittier College—lacked the magnetism of the Steelers quarterback. Nixon was forced to resign in 1974, the same year as the Steelers' first championship season.

THE STEELER DYNASTY: 1969–1991

together. You put a running game together. You control the clock. You let your defense keep you in the game. You put sustaining drives together. You do play action. Then you go deep when people come up to stop the run. That's how we played. That's it; nothing fancy."

This "nothing fancy" quarterback wound up as one of the greatest QBs of all time. Leading the Steelers from 1970 to '83, Bradshaw completed 2,025 passes for 27,989 yards and 212 touchdowns—while rushing for 2,257 yards and 32 scores.

Then there were the Super Bowl victories—IX, X, XIII, and XIV. In Super Bowl X, Bradshaw's 64-yard touchdown pass to Lynn Swann (who made an acrobatic catch) is considered one of the greatest in NFL history.

In Super Bowl XIII, which followed his 1978 MVP season—in which he passed for more than 2,900 yards and a league-leading 28 touchdowns—Bradshaw took MVP honors. He completed 17 of 30 passes for a then-record 318 yards and four TDs. As Super Bowl MVP in XIV, he passed for 309 yards and two touchdowns.

"I just wanted to win," he said. "We won. I did my job. Isn't that it?"

No, it's not. Like many of his teammates, Bradshaw had an indomitable will to succeed—to play to his best and better. Witness his last game on December 10, 1983.

At the end of the previous season, 1982, Bradshaw was more or less finished. Even though he led the league with 17 touchdown passes during that strike-shortened season, his elbow required off-season surgery, and it was uncertain whether he'd return. He did, for a final bow.

With two games left in the 1983 season, the Steelers were 9–5 and needed to beat the Jets—and the vaunted New York Sack Exchange—to lock up a postseason trip. Noll called on Bradshaw one last time. Just hand the ball off, Bradshaw was instructed. Bradshaw nodded. Two touchdown passes later, the Steelers had clinched a playoff berth.

After the game, lineman Tunch Ilkin asked Bradshaw about running the ball.

"Tunch," Bradshaw said, "I ain't no mailman. I'm a gunslinger. I just wanted to show everybody I could do it because nobody thought I could."

For Terry Bradshaw, the country boy act masked his on-field intelligence and passionate drive to win. Drafted No. 1 overall in 1970, Bradshaw had a gunslinger's nerve and safecracker's hands. In his fifth year, the Steelers were champions.

PITTSBURGH STEELERS YESTERDAY & TODAY

The Immaculate Reception

All the effort that Chuck Noll & Co. had exerted in rebuilding the Steelers finally netted results in 1972. The key was four years of incredible drafts. Joe Greene, L. C. Greenwood, and Jon Kolb arrived in 1969. Terry Bradshaw and Mel Blount were selected the following year. The 1971 draft brought Frank Lewis, Jack Ham, Steve Davis, Dwight White, Larry Brown, Ernie Holmes, and Mike Wagner.

Then Franco Harris arrived in 1972. How important was he? "In the [eight] years before we drafted Franco," Art Rooney Jr. wrote in his book *Ruanaidh: The Story of Art Rooney and His Clan,* "there were no winning seasons. From the beginning to the end of his career as a Steeler—twelve years in all—there were no losing seasons."

"We tried to draft intelligent people," Chuck Noll said.

To do so, the Steelers administered intelligence tests to players, sent for their college transcripts, and even looked at the courses they took. For three years under Noll, the team lost. Then in 1972, the Steelers won more games than any team in franchise history. They went 11–3 and finished in first place for the first time in 25 years.

That gave the Steelers the right to face the Oakland Raiders in the AFC playoffs at Three Rivers Stadium. Although Pittsburgh had beaten the Raiders during the regular season, the men in black were not to be taken lightly. Like the Steelers, they were a tough, hard-hitting team—well balanced and dangerous. As Art Rooney Jr. stated in his book, "the Raiders had a lineup of skilled, veteran bruisers, capable, I thought, of making us look bad."

Not surprisingly, the game turned into a defensive battle. The normally potent Raider offense of Kenny Stabler, Daryle Lamonica, Fred Biletnikoff, Art Shell, and Gene Upshaw played nearly 60 minutes of football against the Steel Curtain defense and came up dry. Finally, with 1:13 left and the Steelers leading 6–0, Stabler scampered 30 yards for a touchdown, and Oakland took the lead 7–6.

When the Steelers got the ball, Bradshaw fired three incomplete passes, and the team faced fourth down on its own 40-yard line with 22 seconds to go. Bradshaw called for a pass, the 66 Circle Option, to get the team within kicking range, but everyone knew it was a long shot. Steelers linebacker Andy Russell said it felt like the game was over.

So bleak were the Steelers' hopes that even the Chief had given up. Head hung, shoulders slumped, Art Rooney Sr. left

> "I FELT SOMEONE HIT ME FROM BEHIND. NEXT THING I KNEW, FRANCO WENT ROARING PAST ME, AND I WONDERED WHAT WAS GOING ON."
>
> —FRENCHY FUQUA, TERRY BRADSHAW'S INTENDED TARGET ON THE IMMACULATE RECEPTION PLAY

The Immaculate Reception remains one of the most famous plays in NFL history. With seconds remaining, Terry Bradshaw's pass ricocheted backward off either Frenchy Fuqua or Jack Tatum. Franco Harris (far right) caught the deflection and ran it in for the winning score.

before the denouement and prepared to give his players his 40th consecutive set of condolences.

The elevator doors banged shut, and the Chief missed the most famous play in football history.

"I always looked for something," Harris said. "Play the situation. Make something happen. Make the big play. I learned early at Penn State to always be around the ball, be around the action. Maybe there'll be a fumble. Maybe I'll throw a block. Because of that attitude, the Immaculate Reception happened."

Bradshaw, scrambling, fired one of his patented armor-piercing passes to John "Frenchy" Fuqua, which instead seemed to hit Oakland strong safety Jack Tatum. Bradshaw slammed his helmet in disgust as the ball fell and fell… until—seemingly out of nowhere—Harris arrived. Franco had trailed the play, as he had done at Penn State. He snatched the ball inches before it hit the ground and raced for the end zone.

"I saw the ball and thought I could catch it," Fuqua recalled in *Steel Dynasty*. "But I felt someone hit me from behind. Next thing I knew, Franco went roaring past me, and I wondered what was going on."

The Raiders claimed that Fuqua touched the ball. If so, the completion should not have counted because two offensive players could not touch a pass consecutively. The officials did not think Fuqua touched the ball, and Frenchy refused to comment.

Amid pandemonium at Three Rivers Stadium, Pittsburgh won 13–7. "The play," Harris said, "just gets bigger every year."

Dubbed the "Immaculate Reception" by a caller to broadcaster Myron Cope, it became Chuck Noll's all-time favorite Steelers moment. "Up until that point," he recalled, "I was the one who believed this was a good football team. That play was a sign that this was a team of destiny."

With the victory, the Steelers went on to play in the AFC championship game. They lost 21–17 to the Miami Dolphins, who were on their way to their legendary undefeated season.

Nevertheless, the Steelers had their victory. At last.

As Terry Bradshaw celebrated the victory, the controversy began. The Steelers claimed that Oakland's Jack Tatum hit the ball, making Harris's catch legal, while the Raiders insisted that Frenchy Fuqua touched it, disqualifying the score. Regardless, it was the Steelers' first-ever playoff win.

Franco Harris eludes Jimmy Warren's tackle en route to his 60-yard Immaculate Reception. It was the perfect home-field ending to Harris's rookie season. The popular, hard-driving running back had rushed for 1,055 yards and captured the fans' imaginations.

PITTSBURGH STEELERS YESTERDAY & TODAY

Drafting to the Super Bowl

When Chuck Noll succeeded Bill Austin as Steelers head coach in 1969, he vowed to do the one thing that coach Buddy Parker had not: build the team through the draft.

Beginning with Joe Greene in '69, Noll transformed a fundamentally bad football team into a good one. Besides looking for athleticism, the Steelers administered intelligence tests to prospective draftees. The Steelers were looking for exceptional people—those who would thrive in the team's new system.

Players such as Terry Bradshaw, Jack Ham, Franco Harris, and Mel Blount made the Steelers competitive, but not championship caliber. Not until 1974, which began with the greatest draft by any team in NFL history, did the Steelers capture their first championship. That was the year that four future Hall of Famers arrived for their first NFL training camp:

It may be the most sought-after ticket among Steelers collectors, the one for Super Bowl IX, at which Pittsburgh won its first NFL championship. Nearly 81,000 fans packed Tulane Stadium on a cloudy, chilly afternoon in New Orleans.

Lynn Swann, John Stallworth, Jack Lambert, and Mike Webster. What they brought—smarts, skill, and exceptional work ethic—put the Steelers over the top.

"The first player we selected in the 1974 draft would be the 21st who was picked overall," Art Rooney Jr. recalled in his book *Ruanaidh*. The Steelers, Rooney wrote, didn't want to "be 'reaching'—taking a chance on a player with what Noll aptly referred to as 'impediments.' [Instead, they would] be looking for 'exceptions'—players deficient in size and/or speed but with qualities not as easy to assess, qualities like intelligence, tenacity, an instinct for the game."

Swann's size seemingly worked against him; he was only 5'11". Lambert was considered too thin to be a linebacker, and Webster was thought to be too small to play center. Yet each man played with heart and smarts.

"In Swann, Stallworth, Lambert, and Webster," Rooney wrote in his book, "we had identified four good draft picks we believed the rest of the teams had underrated, or, in Stallworth's case, overlooked."

"That draft," Mel Blount said, "put us ahead of the league."

The Steelers also got a break from an unexpected source when the NFL Players Association called a strike before training camp. The rookies had the run of the place. Getting unprecedented playing time, the first-year players quickly learned the Steelers system and showed the coaches what they could do.

Quarterback controversy raged through much of 1974. Former Notre Dame star Terry Hanratty (right) was 3-of-26 in three games, Joe Gilliam (left) went 4–1–1 in six starts, and Terry Bradshaw went 5–2 in seven starts—and then 3–0 during the postseason run.

42

THE STEELER DYNASTY: 1969–1991

J. T. Thomas tries to break up a pass to Ahmad Rashad during Pittsburgh's 32–14 win over Buffalo in a 1974 AFC divisional playoff game. Franco Harris scored three times, and the Steelers held superstar running back O. J. Simpson to just 49 yards.

Dying to Play

Perhaps no single moment symbolized the Steelers dynasty more than Dwight White's miraculous appearance in Super Bowl IX.

Aptly called "Mad Dog" for his hard-hitting, trash-talking style, White played defensive end on the Steel Curtain. In January 1975, as the Steelers prepared for the Super Bowl in New Orleans, White lay in a hospital bed with pneumonia. Having lost 20 pounds, he certainly was not expected to play.

On the morning of the game, however, White was on the sidelines, suited up, banging heads with Joe Greene. Defensive coordinator George Perles planned to start White for just one series.

White, however, never came out of the game. He helped limit the Vikings to only 17 yards rushing, and, in fact, recorded the game's first points, sacking Minnesota quarterback Fran Tarkenton for a safety.

After the game, White returned to the hospital for another week.

"I had a lot of pride and made a big contribution that year," White said. "The bottom line: It was too big a game to miss."

Dwight White

Quarterback Terry Bradshaw opened the 1974 season on the bench. With "Jefferson Street" Joe Gilliam piloting the team, the Steelers looked fabulous, winning four and tying one in his first six starts. After Pittsburgh crushed the Colts in the opener 30–0, Gilliam threw 50 passes for 348 yards against Denver in a 35–35 tie. He tanked against the Raiders, going 8-for-31 in a 17–0 loss, but defeated Houston 13–7 the following week.

The Steelers beat the Chiefs in Kansas City 34–24, but for all of Gilliam's aerial finesse, only one touchdown came on a pass. After a 20–16 win over the Browns in Week 6, it appeared that Harris and kicker Roy Gerela would continue to lead the team in scoring.

"Gilliam was a brilliant player," said Andy Russell, as quoted in *Steel Dynasty*. "I mean absolutely, astoundingly good. His arm was as strong as there was. He was an awesome talent. He was leading the league in passing. And Noll benched him."

PITTSBURGH STEELERS YESTERDAY & TODAY

Why? The simple answer is that Gilliam wanted to throw while Noll preferred a ball-control game—hand off to Harris on third-and-five, not heave it downfield.

Suddenly, on a Monday night in October, Bradshaw was back. A 24–17 win over Atlanta that evening marked an irreversible change in the team. With a more balanced attack, the Steelers seemed more sure of themselves. For one thing, Harris was getting the ball more. For another, Lambert was emerging as a brilliant young linebacker.

Believing in themselves more than ever, the Steelers continued to drive toward a third consecutive division title. The Steel Curtain slammed shut on the Eagles, as Pittsburgh defeated Philadelphia 27–0 thanks in part to a 52-yard Blount interception and touchdown.

> "THE ZONE IS NOT A PLACE THAT YOU VISIT VERY OFTEN. YOU'RE LUCKY IF YOU GET THERE ONCE IN YOUR CAREER. THAT'S WHERE WE WERE THAT DAY AS A TEAM. IT WAS A QUIET CONFIDENCE, AND IT LASTED A LONG TIME."
>
> —JOE GREENE, DESCRIBING THE STEELERS' MENTAL STATE DURING THE AFC CHAMPIONSHIP GAME

The Steelers lost to the Bengals 17–10, but at Cleveland the Black and Gold returned to form, winning 26–16, with J. T. Thomas

Fred Biletnikoff couldn't quite catch this pass—ruled incomplete despite alleged interference by J. T. Thomas—in the 1974 AFC championship game. After trailing 10–3, the Steelers scored three touchdowns in the fourth quarter to win 24–13.

No one had ever seen as devastating a defense as the Steel Curtain. As captured in this Walter Iooss Sports Illustrated *photo, the Steelers manhandled Minnesota in Super Bowl IX, limiting the Viking to just 119 yards on the way to a 16–6 victory.*

running back a fumble for the final Steelers touchdown. In New Orleans, Pittsburgh punished the Saints 28–7, with Bradshaw running for a touchdown and Swann returning a punt 64 yards for another.

Still wobbly, the Steelers fell to the Oilers 13–10 at Three Rivers, letting Houston off the carpet just enough for the tying and winning field goals. Closing out the season, the Steelers beat the Patriots 21–17, with Swann hauling in a Bradshaw touchdown pass and L. C. Greenwood dumping Jim Plunkett for a safety. Finally, at Three Rivers, it was payback against the Bengals, 27–3. Pittsburgh finished 10–3–1.

Primed for the playoffs, the AFC Central champs opened at Three Rivers against the Buffalo Bills and superstar halfback O. J. Simpson. With the Stunt 4–3 working to perfection, Joe Greene swallowing the line, and Lambert hitting everything in sight, Simpson gained a measly 49 yards on 15 carries in the 32–14 Steelers rout.

THE STEELER DYNASTY 1969–1991

After the Raiders beat the Dolphins, pundits claimed that the real Super Bowl had already been played. Fired up, the usually unemotional Noll told his players that "the best team is sitting right here in this room."

"That's when I knew," Greene recalled. "Right there. It's the most special thing an athlete can feel. And the most beautiful thing about it is that it lasted two weeks. When he said that, there wasn't anything the Raiders could do to win that game."

Having beaten the Steelers that season, the Raiders tried to bully Pittsburgh. It didn't work. With the score 10–10 in the fourth quarter, Ham intercepted a Kenny Stabler pass and Bradshaw threw to Swann for a touchdown. After a George Blanda field goal cut it to 17–13, J. T. Thomas intercepted a Stabler pass. Harris ran the ball in for a touchdown to cap off a 24–13 victory.

"The zone is not a place that you visit very often," Greene recalled. "You're lucky if you get there once in your career. That's where we were that day as a team."

Then it was off to New Orleans, at Tulane Stadium, to face Minnesota. The Vikings were two-time Super Bowl losers, and both teams were looking for their first Super Bowl victory. The favored Vikings featured the "Purple People Eaters," starring defensive linemen Carl Eller and Alan Page, and wily veteran quarterback Fran Tarkenton.

The Steelers were shaky early on, fumbling the ball and blowing a field goal in the first quarter. But then Dwight White downed Tarkenton for a safety and the game's first score.

After leading 2–0 at the half, the Steelers went up 9–0 on a Harris touchdown. Blount intercepted Tarkenton and Greenwood batted three passes, one of which Greene intercepted. Minnesota recovered a blocked Bobby Walden punt in the end zone to make the score 9–6, but a Bradshaw pass to tight end Larry Brown iced the game, 16–6.

Harris, who ran for 158 yards, was named MVP. The Vikings gained only 119 yards, including 17 on the ground.

It took five years to go from dead last to world champs. When NFL Commissioner Pete Rozelle gave the Lombardi Trophy to Art Rooney Sr., who had lived with 40 years of losers, there wasn't a dry eye in the house.

"We were happy," Joe Greene said. "The Super Bowl was a very sweet victory."

The Steelers' first score in Super Bowl IX made history. After Minnesota quarterback Fran Tarkenton and fullback Dave Osborn botched the handoff, the ball bounced into their own end zone. Dwight White downed Tarkenton for the first-ever Super Bowl safety and a 2–0 lead.

NFL Commissioner Pete Rozelle presented Art Rooney with the Vince Lombardi Trophy after Pittsburgh's Super Bowl victory. Never losing faith in his town or team, the Chief—after owning the team for 42 years—finally had his dream fulfilled.

STEELERS MEMORIES

It was as if the entire city went black and gold overnight. During the dynasty, Steelers bumper stickers were plastered on everything from pickup trucks to rec room walls.

A Pittsburgh brewing company for more than a century, Iron City naturally minted a memorial can for the victorious first Super Bowl. Pictured is the team that won Super Bowl IX in January 1975.

Franco Harris, meet Frank Sinatra. Ol' Blue Eyes himself was inducted as a one-star general into Franco's Italian Army in Palm Springs, California, in 1972.

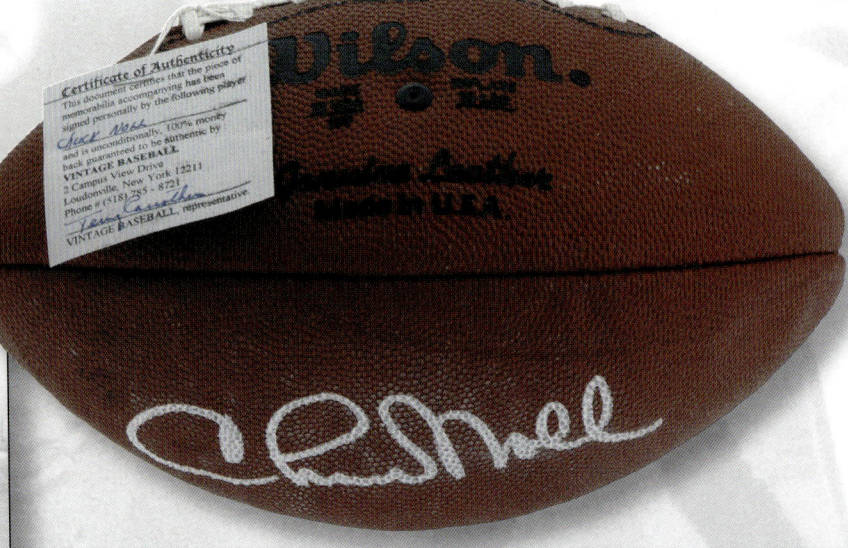

As an NFL head coach, Chuck Noll won 193 regular-season games, the sixth most in the 20th century. An autograph of this NFL legend is highly coveted.

After the Steelers beat Minnesota in Super Bowl IX, a triumphant Terry Bradshaw gave the No. 1 sign at the victory parade in downtown Pittsburgh on January 13, 1975.

Once the Steelers began winning, everybody wanted to get into the act. By 1973, even Royal Crown Cola was producing commemorative Steelers bottles.

When the Steelers won Super Bowl IX, the now-defunct *Pittsburgh Press* added color—then a rarity in the newspaper business—to the front page to celebrate the victory.

Soon after the Super Bowl IX rings were cast, knockoffs of all kinds made the rounds. One of the more valuable items was a look-alike pendant, pictured here.

"The Soul of This Team"

He blocked for Lydell Mitchell at Penn State, so perhaps 6'2", 230-pound running back Franco Harris wouldn't get many handoffs in the NFL. Yet the Steelers liked him—his strength and smarts—and made Harris their No. 1 draft choice (13th overall) in the 1972 draft.

Early on, Harris seemed slow and tentative—until the preseason game against Atlanta when he had a left-side route. When the hole didn't open, Harris turned at full speed, dashed through the middle, cut to the sideline, and galloped 75 yards for a touchdown.

"We got us one!" Joe Greene bellowed. Mean Joe later recalled: "That was the happiest moment I ever had in Steelers football."

"I had vision, anticipation," Harris said. "My strong suit was reading. I could read certain situations quickly, I could see a guy flinch and know what was going to develop. I was also good at reacting. If something didn't happen a certain way, I had the quickness to react."

Playing for the Steelers from 1972 to '83, Harris—Dan Rooney said—"was a winner, the guy who brought it to fruition. Not only was a he a great player, he was the soul of this team."

"He was the single most important guy," Greene said, "who got us that rough first down, who kept the ball when we needed it, the guy the team rallied around."

Harris rushed for 1,000 yards eight times, and he racked up 47 100-yard games. A nine-time Pro Bowler, he rushed for 158 yards in Super Bowl IX, netting MVP honors.

"The fun of running was... making something happen to make the team successful," he said. "I always looked for the big play. Play the situation. Have fun with it. That's why I enjoyed it for so long. I had fun."

After his "breakthrough" rookie season in 1972, Franco Harris appeared on the cover of Sport *magazine the following fall. Harris's 5.6 yards per carry in 1972 led all NFL running backs and remained a career high.*

Franco Harris read plays quickly, adapted to them, and ran hard. Remarkably reliable during his 12-year Steelers career, he set an NFL record with eight 1,000-yard rushing seasons, breaking Jim Brown's record of seven.

The Rock Could Block

As a Steelers rookie in 1968, Rocky Bleier was slow, small, and marginal. He had been a sentimental pick of the Chief. Not only were both men Irish, but each had grown up above a saloon, yearning to play football.

Shipped off to Vietnam in 1969, Bleier came back with a Bronze Star, a Purple Heart, a bullet wound in his left leg, and a right foot full of shrapnel. After three operations, Bleier's iron will got him back in a Steelers jersey. "I was willing to do everything to make the team," he said.

A starter by 1974, Bleier was a key part of the offense. At first, he achieved fame as Franco Harris's smart, tough blocker. Then came his own 1,000-yard rushing performance in 1976. "It was a glorious achievement," he said, "because it wasn't expected."

Rocky Bleier

THE STEELER DYNASTY: 1969–1991

A Pair of Jacks

Arriving in 1971 and '74, respectively, Jack Ham and Jack Lambert joined a canny holdover, Andy Russell, as Steelers linebackers.

"Andy Russell, Jack Ham, and Jack Lambert—our linebackers were all 220 pounds, ran 4.5 40s, and were smart as all get-out," Terry Bradshaw said. "Those are the kind of people Chuck [Noll] wanted, because smart people don't make mistakes. They may lack a little bit physically, but they make up for it. They're in the right position because they're so smart."

"Jack Ham was a brilliant player," Russell said. "He didn't make any mistakes, knew the game, and anticipated well. Plus, he was an explosive talent, probably the fastest Steeler in five yards—an incredible explosion off the blocker. And he'd make it look easy. It was astounding how good he was. He was the best linebacker I ever saw."

"He was the best I ever saw for coverage," former Steelers coach Bud Carson added. "There was nobody like him."

"Jack Ham was so good," Dick Hoak said, "that it got to the point that teams wouldn't throw the ball over there anymore."

Cool, cerebral Ham on one side, fiery, hard-hitting Lambert on the other—bookends and future Hall of Famers. Ham was a six-time first-team All-Pro, while Lambert earned the honor seven times and was named the 1976 NFL Defensive Player of the Year.

"Lambert may have had that image as a wild man," Russell said, "but he killed you with his precision. He was a great anticipator. Read his keys. Took angles away from blockers. Never made a mistake. But what really set him aside as a great middle linebacker was his ability to cover the pass. He was dramatically better than anyone else on the pass. Lambert did things never asked of a middle linebacker—and he did them superbly."

"Jack was very smart," Ham agreed. "Oh, he made a tough hit on somebody, and people said, 'There's that crazy guy out there on the field.' But he was a very intelligent player, and in that sense we were alike. We'd make sure we didn't make a mental error—because at that level it's not the physical things that will beat you. It's the mental breakdowns. In the big game, two or three plays will make the game for you."

"When you start talking about attitude and focus," Noll said, "Jack Lambert is the epitome. He was the most focused individual I've ever had. He'd go on the practice field and there was no nonsense. It was get the job done."

> "LAMBERT MAY HAVE HAD THAT IMAGE AS A WILD MAN, BUT HE KILLED YOU WITH HIS PRECISION."
>
> —FELLOW STEELERS LINEBACKER ANDY RUSSELL

What Hall of Fame linebackers Jack Ham (center) and Jack Lambert (right) lacked in size they made up for in preparation and anticipation.

Defining the ferocity of the 1970s Steelers, Jack Lambert (photographed by Tony Tomsic for Sports Illustrated) appeared as a toothless, snarling demon. Yet his persona masked great intelligence and uncanny precision. Chuck Noll called him the most focused player he ever had.

Inheriting the Throne

How do you succeed a legend?

"I never really tried to be my dad," Dan Rooney said. "I always said I'm going to be me; I'm not going to try to emulate him. So I ran this business a little differently than he did. I didn't try to act like him. I didn't think I should."

A successful scholastic player, Dan was brought up around the Steelers, working at training camp from the time he was a young child. After graduating from Duquesne University in 1955, he was ready to join the club full-time.

"It was not assumed that I would go into the family business," he said. "It wasn't a guarantee. Because in the 1950s, my father wasn't too sure that the Steelers were the world's greatest business."

By 1964, Dan was heading daily operations—signing players, handling the budget, making travel arrangements. In 1975, he became the team's president, a position he held until passing the torch to his son Art Rooney II in 2003. Dan is currently chairman emeritus of the Steelers.

Dan Rooney's ownership style—and his extensive work for the NFL—has been marked by community pride, franchise

Since the days of his youth, when he helped out at the Steelers' training camps, Dan Rooney (left) wanted nothing more than to work for his father's team. Dan began handling daily operations in 1964 and succeeded his father (right) as president in 1975.

Philanthropist and Ambassador

In the old days, Art Rooney Sr. kept his philanthropy close to the vest. No one knows how many down-and-outers he kept going. By contrast, Dan Rooney's generosity is well documented. In Pittsburgh, he contributes to the Holy Family Institute, the Cardinal Wright Regional School, Catholic Charities, the Catholic Youth Association, Duquesne University, St. Vincent College, and others.

Barack Obama and Dan Rooney

Most notably, in 1976 Rooney helped found the American Ireland Fund, which has raised $300 million for peace advocacy and education. He is also the benefactor for the Rooney Prize for Irish Literature.

In 2009, President Barack Obama tapped Rooney to be the U.S. ambassador to Ireland. "American diplomacy is the best chance for peace in the world," Rooney told the Senate Foreign Relations Committee, "and Ireland is its shining example."

stability, and consistent leadership. An able, steady-handed owner, he has conducted himself with patience, decency, and dignity.

"Dan's never received the credit for what's happened here," former club official Tom Donahoe said. "Not only has he lived in the shadow of his father, he's lived in the shadow of coach Noll. But a successful franchise is a team effort. If you don't have a good, solid owner, it doesn't make any difference what else you have. You're never going to be successful."

"I had my father for a long time," Dan Rooney says. "It was really something to go in and talk with him. It gave me the feeling of being on solid ground."

THE STEELER DYNASTY: 1969–1991

Terry's Targets

They came together in that remarkable 1974 draft, two Hall of Fame receivers—the glamour boy, acrobatic Lynn Swann from Southern Cal, and the lunch-bucket plugger, John Stallworth from Alabama A&M.

Together, they changed Steelers history.

For more than 40 years, the Steelers had never been a passing team. They generally followed the old football axiom that when you throw the ball, one of three things will happen—and two of them are bad.

By the early 1970s, the team had decent receivers but no one with great leaping ability or magical hands—no one to snag 'em for Terry Bradshaw. Then came Swann, a trained dancer (including ballet).

"Swann's big thing was his great timing and his ability to jump," said defensive back turned super scout Jack Butler. "He knew when to go up. Great hands, great eye-hand coordination. Plus, he was a tough little guy and took a lot of big hits."

The Steelers, Swann said, "were known primarily as a strong defensive team. Very physical, with a conservative offense, a running attack. When John and I arrived, the Steelers became dangerous throwing the football... John and I established a reputation that if Bradshaw put the ball in the air, we could hurt you very badly with only three to five catches in the ballgame."

Hurt, he did. In just nine seasons (1974–82), Swann led the team in receptions five times, amassing 5,462 receiving yards and 51 touchdown catches.

"I can't say that Bradshaw intentionally threw passes high so I could outleap coverage," Swann said. "The go-to person isn't the guy who is open all the time. He's the person that, in the clutch situation, you know you can go to high, and if he can't make the catch, it won't get picked off."

As famous as Swann was for making circus catches, Stallworth became known for his workmanlike dependability. "Swann was from Southern California," Stallworth said. "I was from Huntsville, Alabama. There's the difference in our styles. I was steady and consistent in getting open and catching the vast majority of passes. Maybe I didn't do that with a lot of panache, but I got the job done. I was able to come up with the big catch when we needed the big catch."

Playing 14 years (1974–87), Stallworth set Steelers career records for receptions (537), receiving yards (8,723), and touchdowns (63), all later broken by Hines Ward.

"It wasn't flashy," Stallworth said, "but in the context of what the team wanted to accomplish, it was very valuable."

> "SWANN WAS FROM SOUTHERN CALIFORNIA. I WAS FROM HUNTSVILLE, ALABAMA. THERE'S THE DIFFERENCE IN OUR STYLES."
>
> —JOHN STALLWORTH

In 14 seasons with the Steelers, John Stallworth set team career records for receptions, receiving yards, and touchdown catches. Here, he outraces the Cowboys defense during a 75-yard touchdown reception in Super Bowl XIII.

PITTSBURGH STEELERS YESTERDAY & TODAY

Corralling the Cowboys

Super Bowl X in January 1976 was a game for the ages. America's Team versus America's Nightmare; silver-and-blue heroes versus black-and-gold dementos. All-around good guy and Naval Academy star Roger Staubach versus toothless, snarling Jack Lambert.

When 11 Cowboys lined up on the field, fans could imagine their 34 teammates helping little old ladies across the street. With the Steelers, they figured the rest of the squad was in the parking lot stripping cars.

Clint Eastwood and John Wayne were cowboys. Steelworkers worked in mills and mines.

Dallas was part of the new go-go South, new money, a new morality, and oh those cheerleaders—cute and wholesome, yet barely wearing enough to keep it legal.

Pittsburgh was the Buckle of the Rust Belt, whose short-lived cheerleaders had dressed with the panache of nuns— and who had been dropped because they were considered distractions.

But the Steelers, after their Super Bowl IX victory, were a team transformed in 1975. "The toughest part of winning the Super Bowl," L. C. Greenwood recalled, "was that we had to go out the next year and play every game like it was the Super Bowl. Every Sunday, every team was after us. But that's how we surpassed a lot of teams at the time, how we were able to make it two years in a row."

The Steelers kicked off the season in San Diego, where they steamrolled the unprepared and overmatched Chargers 37–0. The next week, the Bills led 10–0 at the half after a Terry Bradshaw fumble was returned for a touchdown. Buffalo went up 23–0 before Franco Harris finally scored twice, but the Bills ran away with it 30–21.

As reigning Super Bowl champions in 1975, the Steelers knew that teams would be gunning for them. And they were ready. Thanks largely to the running of Rocky Bleier (20) and Franco Harris (32), Pittsburgh finished 12–2 and outscored its opponents 373–162.

Including the postseason, the 1975 Steelers won 14 of their final 15 games.

In the 1975 AFC divisional playoffs, the Steelers romped over the Colts 28–10. Here, lineman Steve Furness and linebacker Jack Lambert rough up running back Lydell Mitchell. In the fourth quarter, linebacker Andy Russell returned a fumble 93 yards for a touchdown.

THE STEELER DYNASTY: 1969–1991

From there, Pittsburgh ripped off 11 wins in a row. In Cleveland, the Steelers put up 28 points before the Browns scored, and they cruised 42–6. Week 4 at Three Rivers saw the Broncos drew first blood with a field goal, but two Lynn Swann catches and a Roy Gerela field goal quickly made it 17–3. Denver managed two more field goals, but the final was 20–9.

> "WE WERE THE TEAM THAT EVERYBODY HAD TO DEAL WITH. THAT WAS THE YEAR THAT NOBODY WAS GOING TO GET IN OUR WAY."
>
> —JOE GREENE, ON THE 1975 STEELERS

The next week at Three Rivers, Chicago opened the scoring with a field goal before the Steelers reeled off 34 unanswered points. Harris, Rocky Bleier, and Bradshaw all ran the ball for touchdowns.

Facing a tougher contest at Green Bay, the Steelers depended on field position, Gerela, and a 94-yard Mike Collier kick return to nip the Packers 16–13. Against the Bengals at Riverfront, Pittsburgh gave up a field-goal lead, then scored three touchdowns (including two Swann catches) and a field goal. Cincinnati's Kenny Anderson connected for three TDs, but Bradshaw ran one in and the Steelers prevailed 30–24.

The 1975 AFC championship game was played on a frozen field at Three Rivers Stadium. Led by Jack Lambert, who recovered three fumbles, the Steelers beat Oakland 16–10. Here, linebacker Andy Russell sacks quarterback Kenny Stabler.

A Painful Price to Pay

The 1970s Steelers achieved enormous success, but they paid for it with their bodies.

In the Super Bowl years, no player emerged unscathed. Terry Bradshaw suffered a brutal separated shoulder. Both of Lynn Swann's concussions left him unconscious, and physicians warned him that another concussion might permanently disable him. The cartilage in Mike Webster's knee was so damaged that his leg had to be taped so it wouldn't bend. Mike Wagner suffered three cracked neck vertebrae. On one interception, he recalled, he was hit so hard that "they could hear me scream in the upper deck."

Even the seemingly invincible Joe Greene writhed in pain. A nerve in his neck was pinched so badly that he could barely lift 25 pounds. "It wasn't a good time," he said. "Going through the injury and not being out with the team was very painful."

"One thing I always wanted," L. C. Greenwood added, "was to be able to play one game when I wasn't hurt, when there was nothing wrong with me. Because I never played where my ankle or my shoulder or my knee or my back or my hand wasn't hurt."

The Oilers trailed 10–0 in the first quarter at Three Rivers and tried to play catch-up against the Steel Curtain. Although Houston made it interesting, tying the game in the fourth quarter, the Steelers emerged triumphant, winning 24–17. Kansas City was no match the following week, losing to Pittsburgh 28–3.

In the Astrodome, Dwight White sacked Houston's Dan Pastorini for a safety. After an Oilers field goal, the Steelers responded with touchdowns by Harris, Swann, and John Fuqua in a 32–9 victory.

Against the Jets at Shea Stadium, the Steelers put up 20 straight points before allowing Joe Namath & Co. a fourth-quarter score. The final: 20–7. Against the Browns in Pittsburgh, Bradshaw connected twice with Swann, Harris ran two in, and the game ended 31–17.

53

PITTSBURGH STEELERS YESTERDAY & TODAY

It was the all-time NFL circus catch, with Lynn Swann demonstrating his remarkable grace and athleticism. Tripping over Cowboys cornerback Mark Washington, Swann still made the 53-yard catch, which helped him earn Super Bowl X MVP honors.

The Steelers put on another show when the Bengals came to town. Swann caught a touchdown pass and defensive back J. T. Thomas ran in a lateral from Jack Lambert, who had recovered a Cincinnati fumble. The Bengals scored twice, but it was all Steelers, 35–14.

Out in Los Angeles in the season finale, the 11–2 Rams had the Steelers' number. The score was knotted at 3–3 when the "Polish Rifle," Ron Jaworski, ran in a fourth-quarter touchdown for a 10–3 Rams victory.

Nevertheless, the Steelers' 12–2 record was the best in the AFC and the greatest in team history. Their point differential (+211) was the best in the NFL since the undefeated Dolphins in 1972.

"Once we got into it," Joe Greene said about the season, "the offense started to get as good as the defense. Then we were the best team for the entire season. We were the team that everybody had to deal with. That was the year that nobody was going to get in our way."

Pittsburgh romped over the Colts in the playoffs 28–10, with Harris, Bleier, and Bradshaw running for Steelers scores. So did linebacker Andy Russell, who returned a fumble 93 yards. Harris rushed for 153 yards, one less than the entire Baltimore offense.

With the Raiders in town, the AFC championship game was played on a field frozen under a wind chill of –12. The Steelers, spurred by Jack Lambert's three fumble recoveries, prevailed 16–10. In an unforgettable moment, Greene carried Swann off the field after he had been belted unconscious by Raiders defensive back George Atkinson.

Suffering a concussion, Swann spent two days in the hospital and became the Super Bowl X pregame story. He remained dizzy but worked out lightly. Would he play? Could he take the hits? Would he be used as a decoy?

Pittsburgh would face the Cowboys in Miami. Would Dallas's flex defense negate the Steelers' offense, and would its play-action, shotgun-style offense bamboozle the Steel Curtain?

"They were a team we respected," John Stallworth recalled in *Steel Dynasty*. "They had a lot of talent and they were very well coached.... There was a very distinct difference in our styles. We were very much a punch-you-in-the-mouth football team, and they were finesse."

Early fears seemed justified, as a couple of botched plays gave Dallas a 7–0 lead. With the score 10–7 Cowboys, and Dallas on the Steelers' 20, the Steel Curtain woke up. First, a two-yard loss. Then on subsequent plays, Greenwood sacked Staubach for a 12-yard loss and White sacked him for a 10-yard loss.

Swann proceeded to rouse the nation with one of the most memorable plays in Super Bowl history. Both Swann and Cowboys cornerback Mark Washington skied high to catch a

THE STEELER DYNASTY: 1969–1991

The bigger the game, the better L. C. Greenwood played. In Super Bowl X, he sacked Roger (the supposed "Dodger") Staubach four times, including one that forced a fumble on the game's first play from scrimmage. The Steelers logged seven sacks in all.

Bradshaw bomb. Swann, displaying phenomenal concentration and body control, tipped the ball and—while falling on Washington—hauled in the pigskin for a 53-yard gain.

Gerela attempted a field goal to tie, but missed. When Cowboys safety Cliff Harris taunted Gerela by patting him on the helmet, an enraged Jack Lambert picked up Harris and dumped him.

Dallas led 10–7 at intermission, but the second half was all Pittsburgh. Reggie Harrison blocked a Cowboys punt, and the ball bounced through the end zone for a Steelers safety. A Gerela field goal, a Mike Wagner interception, and another field goal put the Steelers ahead 15–10. Bradshaw's 64-yard TD pass to a leaping Swann gave Pittsburgh a 21–10 lead.

Staubach, "Captain Comeback," orchestrated one late touchdown drive and nearly a second one in the final seconds.

The man who had thrown the original "Hail Mary" pass attempted another. But his final heave into the end zone was batted by Wagner into the arms of safety Glen Edwards for an interception.

Swann, who had lain unconscious just two weeks earlier, proved to be much more than a decoy in the big game. He caught four passes for 161 yards to earn the Super Bowl MVP Award.

A day after the Super Bowl, fans swarmed the airport, lined the Parkway into town, and mobbed tiny Market Square to celebrate the Steelers' second Super Bowl victory. Here, coach Chuck Noll raises the Vince Lombardi Trophy for all to see.

PITTSBURGH STEELERS YESTERDAY & TODAY

The Steel Curtain

In the Steel Dynasty's early days, it was the Steelers' defense—especially the linemen, the Steel Curtain—that won games for the Black and Gold.

Or, as a furious Joe Greene once told a fidgety Terry Bradshaw: "Just don't fumble the ball. We'll win the game."

"In the '70s," Dan Rooney said, "the Pittsburgh Steelers played the best defense that has ever been played." It all began with the Steel Curtain: tackles "Mean" Joe Greene and Ernie "Fats" Holmes, and defensive ends Dwight "Mad Dog" White and L. C. "Hollywood Bags" Greenwood.

"The four of us together had a great time," said Greenwood. "We didn't care who we played against. The better they were, the better we reacted against them. We were in sync. We had goals and objectives. We knew what we wanted to do—and what we had to do."

"We all wanted to win very badly, especially when things were so difficult for us," Greene said about his early years. "We were all very, very competitive. We were getting beat on a regular basis—and nobody liked it. The only way to go was forward. That was the only way we wanted to go."

> "WE'D LINE UP AND SAY, 'MEET YOU AT THE QUARTERBACK.'"
> —STEEL CURTAIN DEFENSIVE END L. C. GREENWOOD

Greene and Greenwood came in 1969, White and Holmes in '71. "Mad Dog" White earned his nickname because of his ferocious intensity. He logged 46 career sacks and made the Pro Bowl in 1972 and '73. After being cut from the team in 1971, the 300-pound Holmes made the squad in 1972 and subsequently crushed everything that came his way.

The 6'6" Greenwood, a hunch pick in the 10th round of the 1969 draft, used his great reach to bat down passes (three in Super Bowl IX alone). Until Jason Gildon moved ahead of him, Greenwood held the all-time Steelers sack record with 73.5—not including the four deckings of Roger Staubach in Super Bowl X. Greenwood made a fashion statement as well, dazzling Three Rivers with his famous gold shoes.

The last spoke in the wheel was assistant coach George Perles, who arrived in 1972. "We had a group understanding that we had to stop the running game," Perles said. Inventing the Stunt 4–3, Perles slanted Greene to eat up two or three offensive linemen. Greenwood stuffed the tackle, and the linebackers rambled at will. "The Stunt 4–3 freed Jack Lambert up," defensive coach Bud Carson recalled, "allowing him to take advantage of his natural talents."

Their job: shut 'em down. The most devastating defensive line in NFL history, the Steel Curtain—L. C. Greenwood, Joe Greene, Ernie Holmes, and Dwight White (left to right)—combined determination, strength, and smarts to obliterate opposing offenses.

"Until other teams found out what we were doing," former assistant coach Dick Hoak said, "it was tough for them to run the ball against us." In the 1974 postseason, for example, Pittsburgh held its opponents to 146 yards rushing: Buffalo 100, Oakland 29, and Minnesota 17.

"We worked together extremely well," Greenwood recalled. "We'd line up and say, 'Meet you at the quarterback.' I felt sometimes when we needed a big play, I could take a chance. I could go out of the original defensive structure because I knew where Joe, Lambert, and Ham would be. I knew Ernie'd be there. Dwight would be talking plenty of stuff. Joe would be destroying things. I'd be running till the whistle blew."

"There were some synergies there," White agreed. "Good chemistry. We were confident in our own talents. And we executed very well together."

"That was our job. Shut 'em down," White continued. "'You come to Pittsburgh, don't even try it. You're going to lose the game, and we're going to dominate it.' It was almost arrogance, but as Dizzy Dean said, 'It ain't braggin' if you can do it.' And we did it."

As the Steelers kept winning, and the defense proved more devastating every week, the Steel Curtain became a national phenomenon. Capturing the popular imagination, the front four made the cover of Time *magazine in December 1975.*

A haven for fan-made banners, Three Rivers Stadium was born in 1970, when the Steel Curtain began to dominate the NFL. During the dynasty, numbers 78, 63, 75, and 68 helped bring victories in Super Bowls IX, X, XIII, and XIV.

"No One Could Move the Sticks"

From 1972 to '79, the Steelers rained pain on opposing ball carriers. If by chance the running back made it past the Steel Curtain, and if he could elude linebackers Jack Ham, Jack Lambert, and Andy Russell, he still found himself amid hostile company. Cornerback Mel Blount and strong safety Donnie Shell, supported by free safety Mike Wagner and corner J. T. Thomas, put the hurt on backs who had thought they had gotten lucky.

The Steeler D's legendary reputation is supported by the numbers. From 1972 to '79, Pittsburgh ranked among the NFL's top eight every year in fewest yards per game. They led the league in that category in 1974 and again in '76.

In 1976, the Steelers also led the NFL in fewest points per game—a mere 9.9 on average. After a wobbly start, Pittsburgh ripped off nine straight victories, plus a playoff win against the Colts. Those ten games included five shutouts. "Shutouts in the NFL are unheard of," Andy Russell said. "No field goals?"

Not many points, either. Until the Colts scored two touchdowns, the Steelers gave up 28 points in nine-plus games. "No one," Russell said, "could move the sticks."

STEELERS MEMORIES

Terry Bradshaw's most popular spouse (of three) was All-American sweetheart JoJo Starbuck, a national champion and Olympic ice skater. Her marriage to Bradshaw lasted from 1975 to '83.

What good would any victory be without audio clips? In the days before MP3 players and YouTube, phonograph records did the trick, including this one of Super Bowl X.

Fans have gobbled up anything Steelers related, including a signed, special-edition Steel Curtain jersey, which features the numbers of Messrs. Holmes, Greenwood, Greene, and White.

On July 23, 1976, the Steelers played the College All-Stars in Chicago. Due to stormy weather, the game was called in the third quarter with the Steelers up 24–0. The College All-Star Game, which began in 1934, was never played again.

Jack Ham, the thinking man's linebacker, was celebrated in many ways, including this collectible figurine.

Another Super Bowl victory, another parade. As *The Pittsburgh Press* reported, Pittsburghers paid homage to the Steelers after their thrilling victory in Super Bowl X.

Toothless, snarling, screaming linebacker Jack Lambert was known as "Jack Splat," "Jack the Ripper," and "Count Dracula in Cleats." Those in his fan club were equally "loony."

In June 1975, *Sports Illustrated* honored Rocky Bleier, who overcame Vietnam War wounds to help lead the Steelers to four Super Bowl victories.

With the dynasty came something new for Steeler Nation—replica jerseys. Signed jerseys, such as the one here by Jack Lambert, are premium items among collectors.

The Black Menace

Thanks to the Oakland Raiders, Pittsburgh's 1976 season started and ended miserably. For Week 1, the two-time defending Super Bowl champions had to fly cross-country to Oakland to face the best and baddest team in the NFL.

Coached by John Madden and owned by tough guy Al Davis, the Raiders featured such bruisers as Art Shell, Gene Upshaw, George Atkinson, and Jack "The Assassin" Tatum.

The roots of the Steelers-Raiders rivalry ran deep, beginning with the AFL-NFL merger when bad blood brewed between the Rooneys and Davis. The rivalry was fueled by Chuck Noll, who had worked as a Davis assistant at San Diego—and didn't like it. From 1972 through '76, the Raiders and Steelers bashed helmets in the playoffs every single year.

After the Steelers beat Oakland in the 1972 playoffs with the Immaculate Reception—which the Raiders maintained was an illegal catch—the Silver and Black took their revenge in the 1973 playoffs, whipping the Steelers 33–14.

Along the way, the Steelers alleged that the Raiders led the league in dirty tricks—watering the Oakland Coliseum into mud to slow runners, slathering Vaseline on jerseys to hinder tackling, and using under-inflated footballs to shorten kicks.

In the 1974 AFC championship game, the Steelers put down the Raiders 24–13. They again met in the conference championship game the following year. The Steelers prevailed 16–10, but not before Atkinson collared Lynn Swann around the neck and threw him to the ground, rendering him unconscious. Joe Greene, who carried Swann off the field, recalled in *Steel Dynasty:* "I looked at the Raiders as being the bullies on the block."

In the 1976 season opener against the Raiders, Swann was 15 yards from Terry Bradshaw's pass to Franco Harris when Atkinson drilled him again. "A devastating blow," John Stallworth said. Chuck Noll had more to say about the matter. "You have a criminal element in all aspects of society," he seethed after the game. "Apparently, we have it in the NFL, too."

Egged on by Davis, Atkinson filed a $2 million slander suit.

The Steelers' 1976 team may have been their best ever. After starting the season 1–4, they closed with nine straight victories. Overall in the regular season, they outscored their opponents 342–138. After blowing out the Colts at Baltimore 40–14 in the first round of the playoffs, Pittsburgh traveled back to Oakland for the AFC championship game. The Raiders, who had finished 13–1 that season, cruised to an easy 24–7 victory and won the Super Bowl that year.

In July 1977, after hearing testimony for two weeks, it took a jury four hours to find Chuck Noll not guilty.

> "YOU HAVE A CRIMINAL ELEMENT IN ALL ASPECTS OF SOCIETY. APPARENTLY, WE HAVE IT IN THE NFL, TOO."
>
> —CHUCK NOLL, ON THE OAKLAND RAIDERS

Terry Bradshaw nearly lost his head to Otis Sistrunk, who sacked the Steelers quarterback for an eight-yard loss in the 1976 AFC championship game. The Steelers lost to the hated Raiders 24–7, ending Pittsburgh's hopes for a third consecutive Super Bowl.

THE STEELER DYNASTY: 1969–1991

Game Day at Three Rivers

When Three Rivers Stadium was reduced to rubble on February 11, 2001, it took with it 31 seasons of Steelers memories (and a 182–73 home record). For many, those highlights came flooding back two months prior, on December 16, 2000, as the Steelers played their last game in the place that, as Chuck Noll remembered, "was our first home. Three Rivers gave us a place to practice, a place to play. It was a big part of our identity."

It was the difference between night and day—from dank, dark Forbes Field and the old Pitt Stadium to the colorful, modern, multipurpose Three Rivers Stadium.

Built back in the trolley era, neither Forbes Field nor Pitt Stadium had dedicated parking. Three Rivers, by contrast, had an ocean of space, perfect for the latest craze—tailgating. People showed up hours before the 1:00 kickoff for barbecue, brewskis, and a bit of pickup football.

Inside, at least some of the color-coded red, yellow, and orange seats were under shelter. Luxury boxes ringed the field, and the two-story Allegheny Club welcomed those who preferred their football behind glass. Finally, Jerome Bettis remembered, "it was a loud, noisy type of place. We capitalized on that—raising a ruckus, the crowd really fired up. That was good for us."

During the Me Decade of the 1970s, costumes were customary—helmets for Franco's Italian Army, the gorilla suit for Gerela's Gorillas. Fans came in T-shirts and jerseys, waved Terrible Towels, and hung homemade jerseys everywhere.

After the last game ever played at Three Rivers, a 24–3 trouncing of Washington, current and retired players milled around the field. They lingered for a long while, shaking hands with fans and sharing precious memories. It was hard to say goodbye.

It gave the team a major-league identity—and the fans their first true venue. Three Rivers Stadium, home to the Steelers for 31 seasons (1970–2000), was a place for tailgating, Franco's Italian Army, Gerela's Gorillas, and a sea of Terrible Towels.

Franco's Italian Army

It began on a whim and spread like wildfire.

In 1972, local baker Tony Stagno, who was proud of Franco Harris's Italian heritage (on his mother's side), invented Franco's Italian Army. This enthusiastic group of *paisonos* attended games wearing army helmets with Harris's number on them. The most famous inductee: Frank Sinatra, at a team practice in Palm Springs, California.

For a while, it seemed that every player had a club of his own—Frenchy's Foreign Legion, Bradshaw's Brigade, Gerela's Gorillas, Ham's Hussars, and so on.

"The spirit of the town was incredible," Harris said. "Franco's Italian Army was a big part of that. Bringing in the fans, and getting them behind us—I really enjoyed it."

PITTSBURGH STEELERS YESTERDAY & TODAY

Lucky XIII

After their back-to-back championship seasons in 1974 and '75, the Steelers juggernaut continued to roll—just not to the Super Bowl. The Black and Gold finished 10–4 in 1976, the year that both Franco Harris and Rocky Bleier each rushed for 1,000 yards and the defense posted five shutouts, but they fell to the Raiders 24–7 in the AFC championship game. Terry Bradshaw aired it out more in 1977, but the results were disappointing—a 9–5 record and an opening-round playoff loss to Denver.

In 1978, however, the Steelers put it all together with a well-balanced offensive attack and the best defense in the league. Football historians rate the 1978 Steelers, who finished the regular season at 14–2 and then stormed through the playoffs, as one of the greatest teams of all time.

The '78 campaign began in Buffalo, with Pittsburgh easily defeating the Bills 28–17. Bradshaw fired TD passes to John Stallworth and Theo Bell, and Harris and Sidney Thornton ran for touchdowns. The Seahawks didn't stand a chance in the Steelers' home opener, as Lynn Swann, Harris, and Thornton scored in a 21–10 victory. Week 3 seemed like little more than a scrimmage—at least for the Steelers. Against the Bengals at Riverfront, the Steel Curtain was a monster, holding Cincinnati to a single field goal as the Steelers cruised 28–3.

The archrival Browns journeyed to Three Rivers looking for an upset. In a tight defensive struggle, with both end zones seemingly off limits, kickers Roy Gerela and Don Cockroft kicked three field goals apiece, including two by Gerala in the fourth quarter that made the score 9–9 and forced overtime. Then came the Play of the Year. The usually conservative Chuck Noll unleashed a gadget play—an old-style, razzle-dazzle flea flicker. After the Steelers flipped the ball back and forth in the backfield, Bradshaw tossed a 37-yard touchdown pass to Bennie Cunningham. The stadium erupted as the Steelers won 15–9.

Feeling nothing short of invincible, the 4–0 Steelers took on the Jets at Shea Stadium. Pittsburgh went up 28–10 before settling for a 28–17 victory, with Bradshaw throwing two touchdown strikes to Swann and another to Stallworth. Back home versus Atlanta, the Steelers put up 31 consecutive points—Bleier running for two, Bradshaw running for one, Stallworth catching the fourth—before Atlanta finally scored. Final: 31–7.

Lynn Swann hauls in a pass during the Steelers' 34–5 triumph over Houston in the 1978 AFC championship game. Playing in a freezing rain, Franco Harris, Rocky Bleier, Lynn Swann, and John Stallworth did what the Oilers couldn't—score touchdowns.

THE STEELER DYNASTY: 1969–1991

Pittsburgh improved to 7–0 with a dominating win at Cleveland. Larry Anderson returned a kickoff 95 yards for a touchdown to spark the Steelers, who triumphed 34–14. Everyone in America knew that Houston coach Bum Phillips was gunning for Pittsburgh. On a Monday night in Three Rivers, Earl Campbell's powerhouse legs scored three touchdowns to Swann's two, and the Oilers prevailed 24–17, ending Pittsburgh's dream of a perfect season.

Kansas City nearly pulled an upset the next week. Down 27–17 in the fourth quarter, the Chiefs came roaring back to fall a field goal short of sending the game into overtime. The Steelers won 27–24.

Stallworth in the air... Stallworth makes the catch! Going high, he scored the first touchdown in the first quarter of Super Bowl XIII. The lead seesawed back and forth, as both the Doomsday Defense and Steel Curtain failed to live up to their reputations.

Slip Sliding Away...

In 1978, Houston Oilers coach Bum Phillips said that the road to Super Bowl XIII went through Pittsburgh. While Phillips would prove prophetic, little did he expect that it ran through a Three River Stadium awash in sleet and slush.

On January 7, 1979, the game time temperature for the AFC championship game between Houston and Pittsburgh was 32 degrees. Rain came down as ice and froze everything it touched.

Oilers quarterback Dan Pastorini complained that he couldn't get his footing, feel the ball, or hear himself think. The Steelers intercepted him five times, including a Mel Blount pick that broke the Oilers' backs.

Players slid all over the field, including little-used Steelers running back Jack "The Hydroplane" Deloplaine, who earned his nickname that day. The Steelers led 14–0 after the first quarter and pounded in 17 points near the end of the half. They skated off with a 34–5 victory.

In terms of sheer guts, this game may have been the Steelers' all-time greatest effort. As Chuck Noll said after the game, "Our football team wanted an unconditional surrender. And we got it."

Facing weak opponents, good teams often let down their guard. The lowly New Orleans Saints flew to Pittsburgh and actually led the Steelers at the half 7–3, but the Black and Gold woke up in the third quarter and put 10 unanswered points on the board. The Saints went ahead 14–13 until a 24-yard Bradshaw-to-Bleier pass won the game 20–14.

The Steelers suffered their second and last loss of the season against the Rams in the L.A. Coliseum. With the game scoreless in the third quarter, Swann caught a 14-yard pass from Bradshaw for Pittsburgh's lone tally. The Rams scored a field goal in the third and a touchdown in the fourth to win 10–7.

Disaster nearly struck the next game. With the 1–10 Bengals at Three Rivers, Cincinnati drew first blood with a field goal. Pittsburgh answered with a Bleier touchdown, and the Bengals kicked another three-pointer. The 7–6 halftime score

PITTSBURGH STEELERS YESTERDAY & TODAY

With the Super Bowl tied at 14–14 late in the second quarter, Mel Blount killed a Cowboys drive with an interception. Terry Bradshaw responded by throwing a seven-yard touchdown pass to Rocky Bleier (pictured) with 26 seconds left in the half.

remained the same at the final gun, as fans headed to the exits wondering what had happened to the Steelers' offense.

Flying out to Candlestick Park, the Steelers returned to form on both sides of the ball. A Gerela field goal and two Swann catches gave the Steelers 17 points at the half—unanswered, because the Steel Curtain shut out the 49ers. San Francisco broke though in the third quarter, but Pittsburgh won 24–7. Looking for payback, the Steelers went to the Astrodome, determined to stop Earl Campbell. Though they successfully held the Oilers to a second-quarter field goal, the Steelers were also held in check—just two Gerela field goals and a five-yard pass to Stallworth. Yet it was enough for a 13–3 victory.

It was a different story the following game at Three Rivers. Playing wide open against Baltimore, the Steelers ran up 21 unanswered points before the Colts were able to score. Five Steelers touchdowns were more than enough to beat Baltimore, 35-13. The season ender, at Mile High Stadium, saw the Steelers go up 21-0 at the half—then struggle to stop the smoking Broncos as they scored 17 unanswered points. As the team held Denver on the goal line to preserve the victory, a jaunty Bradshaw asked Noll, "We had 'em all the way, huh, coach?"

After their 14–2 regular-season performance, the Steelers proceeded to crush the Broncos in the playoffs 33–10, as Denver was unable to stop Harris, Stallworth, and Swann. Pittsburgh then dominated the Oilers in the AFC championship game, winning 34–5. The Steelers defense intercepted Dan Pastorini five times, sacked him four times, and recovered four fumbles, while the great Earl Campbell averaged just 2.8 yards a carry.

Super Bowl XIII was a talent show, the last of five played in Miami's Orange Bowl. Quarterback Roger Staubach and Pitt alum Tony Dorsett starred in the backfield for Dallas, and the

Super Bowl XIII was a blood feud, as Pittsburgh and Dallas each sought a third Super Bowl victory.

As great as the 1978 Steelers were, they were lucky as well. In the third quarter, with Dallas down a touchdown 21–14, veteran Cowboys tight end Jackie Smith dropped a sure six-pointer in the Pittsburgh end zone. Afterward, Smith retired.

THE STEELER DYNASTY: 1969–1991

The Steelers, the first team to win three Super Bowls, enjoyed the fitting culmination to the best season in their history. It was a much different ending for Franco Harris than two years earlier, when he was escorted off the field by Oakland police.

Cowboys' Doomsday Defense featured the No. 1 run defense in the NFL. With Ed "Too Tall" Jones, Harvey "Too Much" Martin, and Randy White on the line; linebackers Bob Breunig, D. D. Lewis, and Thomas "Hollywood" Henderson; and defensive backs Cliff Harris and Charlie Waters, it was a tougher Dallas team than the Steelers had faced in Super Bowl X.

Both teams were looking for a then-unprecedented third Super Bowl victory. The appeal of these two teams took the Super Bowl to new heights. The cost of a 30-second commercial was $185,000, 59 percent higher than for Super Bowl XI. NBC intensified the drama before the game by airing *Black Sunday*, a film about a terrorist attack during a Steelers-Cowboys Super Bowl game... in the Orange Bowl.

The game turned into a shootout, with Bradshaw throwing for three touchdowns in the first half—including 28- and 75-yard strikes to Stallworth. He also completed a seven-yard touchdown pass to Rocky Bleier. Bradshaw's fourth TD pass, to Swann, put Pittsburgh up 35–17 with less than seven minutes to play.

Staubach, however, launched another late comeback, sandwiching two touchdown drives around a successful onside kick. But Bleier recovered the second onside kick with seconds remaining, securing a 35–31 Steelers victory.

Despite Henderson's famous gibe—"Bradshaw couldn't spell cat if you spotted him the *c* and the *t*"—it was Terry's year. He won the NFL Player of the Year Award and Super Bowl MVP Award, and his four touchdown throws and 318 passing yards set Super Bowl records.

In the locker room after the game, Chuck Noll said, "This team hasn't peaked yet." To which Mike Webster replied, "Way to put the pressure on, coach."

The Steelers feel at home even when they're on the road. Not only are there Pittsburghers everywhere, but the team's loyal fans travel nationwide to cheer their football heroes, including Miami's Orange Bowl for Super Bowl XIII.

PITTSBURGH STEELERS YESTERDAY & TODAY

The Last Hurrah

If ever a team hid its age and injuries well, it was the 1979 Steelers. The Black and Gold, coming off a record third Super Bowl victory, marched easily through a 12–4 season in '79 and took their eighth consecutive AFC Central title.

Nevertheless, close observers saw the cracks in the wall. The Steelers might go all the way again, they believed, but the dynasty was nearing its end.

Fans witnessed a changing of the guard on Opening Day. Against the Patriots in Foxborough on Monday night, while the Steelers handled New England 16–13, it was Sidney Thornton—not Franco Harris—who scored the team's two touchdowns. Week 2 was a laugher, with the Steelers beating up on the Oilers 38–7 at Three Rivers, and it was Thornton again scoring, while wide receiver Jim Smith (not Lynn Swann or John Stallworth) snagged a Bradshaw pass for an 18-yard touchdown. On the other side of the ball, linebacker Dennis "Dirt" Winston, not Jack Ham, had a 41-yard interception return.

The next week in St. Louis, the Steelers trailed 21–7 in the fourth quarter before coming to life. After Rocky Bleier and tight end Bennie Cunningham scored, a Matt Bahr field goal gave Pittsburgh the victory 24–21. Against the Colts at Three Rivers, the Steelers found it tough going—until Bradshaw's 47-yard pass to Stallworth and 28-yarder to Cunningham brought home a closely fought 17–13 win.

Against Philadelphia, the Steelers broke a scoreless tie in the second quarter with a Thornton touchdown, but the hapless defense watched the Eagles put 17 points on the board. Trailing by ten in the fourth quarter, Bradshaw connected with Stallworth, but it wasn't enough. Pittsburgh tasted defeat 17–14.

Smarting from the loss, the Steelers took it out on the Browns at Cleveland. Pushing their rival's face into the Municipal Stadium mud to the tune of 51 points, Harris, Thornton, Smith, and Cunningham all scored before the Browns answered with their own scoring binge. By the afternoon's end, Cleveland had 35 points, more than the defense should have allowed.

The road to the Super Bowl, Houston coach Bum Phillips said, ran through Pittsburgh. Unfortunately for Bum, the Oilers ran into a roadblock. As seen on this Sports Illustrated *cover, the Steelers stuffed Houston in the 1979 AFC championship game, 27–13.*

In the 1979 divisional playoff against Miami, Jack Ham, Jon Kolb, and Mike Wagner were replaced by Dirt Winston, Ted Petersen, and J. T. Thomas. Undaunted, the Steelers won 34–14. Here, Zack Valentine tackles punter George Roberts.

Watching the tapes, the Bengals couldn't wait for the Steelers to come to Cincinnati. They put up 34 points of their own in a 34–10 bashing. Humiliated, Pittsburgh put a hurt on Denver when the Broncos came to town. Harris rushed for 121 yards and two touchdowns, and the defense held a fine Denver team to just one first-quarter TD. The final: 42–7.

Fans nationwide brought out the popcorn for the Super Bowl XIII rematch, Cowboys vs. Steelers at Three Rivers. The Steel Curtain shut down the Dallas running game, while Harris rumbled for two scores, including a 48-yarder. Pittsburgh won it 14–3. The Steelers improved to 8–2 after routing the Redskins 38–7, with Bradshaw firing four touchdown passes, including a pair to Stallworth and one each to tight ends Randy Grossman and Cunningham.

With a 30–3 trouncing of Kansas City, the Steelers completed a four-game stretch in which they outscored their opponents 124–20. The letdown was inevitable, and Week 12 saw the Steelers stumble against the Chargers at San Diego 35–7. The blame fell on Bradshaw, who threw five interceptions.

The Browns looked for revenge at Three Rivers, and they nearly got it. Cleveland amassed leads of 10–0, 20–6, and 27–13 before the Steelers came back, scoring 17 fourth-quarter points to tie the game at 30. A Matt Bahr 37-yard field goal in OT won the game for Pittsburgh. Bradshaw threw for 364 yards, and Harris rushed for 151. The Steelers closed the season with easy wins over the Bengals (37–17) and Bills (28–0) sandwiched around a 20–17 loss to the Oilers in front of a raucous Monday night crowd in the Astrodome.

Despite a "home" crowd of 104,000 fans at the Rose Bowl, the Los Angeles Rams were 10 ½ point underdogs against the Steelers in Super Bowl XIV. Pittsburgh actually trailed in the fourth quarter, 19–17, before beating the spread with a 31–19 victory.

In the playoffs against 10–6 Miami, Pittsburgh had to play without Jack Ham. Not missing a beat, the Steelers racked up a 20–0 lead in the first quarter on sustained drives of 62, 62, and 56 yards. Final score: 34–14.

In the AFC title game, with Houston down 17–10, Dan Pastorini's sure touchdown pass to Mike Renfro was incorrectly ruled incomplete. Instead of a tie, the Oilers settled for a field goal. The Steelers added ten points and took the title 27–13. The key was controlling Earl Campbell, who was held to 15 yards on 17 carries.

It was on to Pasadena for Super Bowl XIV against the Rams. Although the Steelers looked great after two dominating postseason performances, they were not taking Los Angeles lightly. After all, the Rams enjoyed a 12–1–2 lifetime record over the Steelers. Moreover, the 104,000 Rose Bowl fans made it seem like a Rams home game.

"We Were Tough People"

As a member of Pittsburgh's Steel Curtain from 1971 to '80, Dwight White understood the Steelers' success as well as anyone. Reflecting back, he discussed the attitude that helped the team win four Super Bowls in the decade.

"We all had that same intensity," White said. "We played a lot of games together in all types of conditions. That's how you can tell what your teammates are made of. Everybody's pretty good in September—they're not all beat up and banged up, and the weather's still nice and pretty, and you're fresh.

"But in late December, when it's cold and people are playing hurt, you look at the guy's face in the huddle, you see blood skeetin' out of his nose, and he's all whipped, and this guy's telling you, 'C'mon, babe, suck it up.' That's really what it's all about. It makes your skin crawl.

"We were tough people, and we took great pride in being tough people. I took great pride being from a smoky, dirty city. That was part of our personality. 'We're going to smoke your butt and dirty you up!'

"We'd dominate the situation. And we'd win."

Franco Harris scores on a one-yard run in the second quarter of the Super Bowl. Throughout the game, the lead changed hands five times. Harris ended the scoring with another one-yard run in the fourth quarter.

In addition, former Steelers coaches Bud Carson and Dan Radakovich were part of the Rams staff. As Chuck Noll recalled in *Steel Dynasty,* "There was no question they knew everything we would do."

Unlike previous years, the Steelers knew they were aging. "It was kind of hit-and-miss at times," Joe Greene recalled in the same book. "I could feel it. We had nagging injuries, a harder time recovering after games. Plays that I was making in the past, I wasn't making anymore."

The Rams led at the half 13–10 and in the third quarter 19–17. With the Steelers' backs to the wall, Bradshaw aired out a long pass that Stallworth caught over his shoulder and turned into a 73-yard touchdown reception. With the score 24–19 Steelers, then 31–19 on a Harris TD, Jack Lambert intercepted a ball on the Steelers' 14. Game over. Like the previous year in Miami, Bradshaw netted MVP honors. He completed 14 of 21 passes for 309 yards, including three tosses to Stallworth for 131 yards.

Since 1970, the Steelers had gone from dead last to four Super Bowl victories. In the playoffs against the NFL's finest teams, they went 14–4. Not a bad decade's work.

"There is no question that the values, goodness, ethics, and character of the people associated with this football team had everything to do with its success," Dan Rooney said. "They were good—but there are a lot of good players. A team has to be one. You have to take the various elements that you have, and they all have to come together. That group of people did that. They believed that the success of the team was more important than individual success."

Added former assistant coach George Perles, "It's a tribute to Mr. Rooney, Dan Rooney, Chuck Noll, and Joe Greene that even though we won four Super Bowls, everybody didn't come unglued and think they were stars and start

> "[T]HE VALUES, GOODNESS, ETHICS, AND CHARACTER OF THE PEOPLE ASSOCIATED WITH THIS FOOTBALL TEAM HAD EVERYTHING TO DO WITH ITS SUCCESS."
> —DAN ROONEY

THE STEELER DYNASTY: 1969–1991

bickering for money, prestige, and recognition."

Champions again, the Steelers were nevertheless hobbled by age, riddled with injuries, and flat-out exhausted. The following year, 1980, the reigning Super Bowl champs didn't even make the playoffs.

With the score 24–19 Steelers following Franco Harris's second touchdown, Jack Lambert intercepted a ball on the Steelers' 14 to clinch the game. Since 1970, the Steelers had gone from last place to four Super Bowl victories. As The Sporting News *reported, No. 1 again!*

Trailing the Rams 19–17, Terry Bradshaw fired a pass down the middle. John Stallworth, who outraced the Rams' Rod Perry, caught the ball over his shoulder and sprinted to the end zone for a 73-yard touchdown reception.

It stands as a record unbroken: four Super Bowl victories in six years. As Franco & Co. celebrated in the Steelers locker room, they hardly knew it would be their last NFL title for 26 years.

STEELERS MEMORIES

Even in the 1980s, Steelers pennants flew high. While the Steelers became just another football team, interest in and loyalty to the Black and Gold never waned.

As shown in this Steeler Pride-Pak, Steelers decals celebrated the team's four victories—and looked forward to a fifth. But the reigning Super Bowl champs wouldn't make the play-offs in 1980 or '81.

In Pittsburgh, the mere utterance of the number 32, no matter the context, conjures up images of Franco Harris. This Harris jersey was signed by the man himself.

There are footballs for playing and footballs for displaying. Here, a full-sized NFL-style football is embroidered with symbols of the Steelers' six Super Bowl victories.

Collectors pay top dollar for game-used uniforms. This Steelers helmet, which was worn by Terry Bradshaw, is valued at more than $6,000.

When the Pirates and Steelers won world titles in 1979, *Sports Illustrated* named Willie Stargell and Terry Bradshaw Co-Sportsmen of the Year. Walter Iooss Jr. posed the pair with steelworkers at a local steel mill.

The Pittsburgh Press celebrated the Steelers' third Super Bowl victory with a photo of Terry Bradshaw and JoJo Starbuck and a cartoon of a Super Steeler.

Hailed by *Sports Illustrated* on its January 29, 1979, cover, the Steelers were unprecedented champions—the first three-time winners of the Super Bowl.

Secondary Terrors

It is one thing to achieve greatness; it's another to cause a rule change because of your exceptional abilities. But that is exactly what Steelers Hall of Fame cornerback Mel Blount did.

Selected by Pittsburgh in the third round of the 1970 draft, Blount played at 6'3", 205 pounds. He possessed extraordinary reach and exceptional speed. "He was the best ever to play the game," said former Steelers defensive coordinator Bud Carson. "There's no one who comes close. With Blount's speed, anticipation, height, and reach, nobody could get away from him."

A former wide receiver—meaning he knew where the ball was going and could catch it when it got there—Blount recalled that "my biggest strength was one-on-one man-to-man coverage. I had an advantage with my height and very long arms."

Playing when corners were permitted to hit open receivers, Blount was so devastating that the NFL changed the rule to prevent such collisions.

Blount missed only one game in 14 seasons (1970–83). He earned five Pro Bowl berths, played in four victorious Super Bowls, and was named the NFL Defensive MVP in 1975. He intercepted 57 passes, setting a Steelers record that still stands. His 11 picks in 1975 are the

Steelers cornerback Mel Blount possessed great reach and sprinter speed. Remarkably, Blount did not allow a single touchdown reception during the 1972 season, and in 1975 he led the league with 11 interceptions.

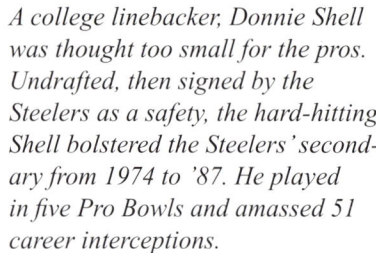

A college linebacker, Donnie Shell was thought too small for the pros. Undrafted, then signed by the Steelers as a safety, the hard-hitting Shell bolstered the Steelers' secondary from 1974 to '87. He played in five Pro Bowls and amassed 51 career interceptions.

most by a Steeler in a single season.

For his part, Donnie Shell was a rare bird, a walk-on who made it big. Shell had played linebacker at all-black South Carolina State well enough to merit enshrinement in the College Football Hall of Fame. But at 5'11" and 198 pounds, he was way too small to play linebacker in the pros. Some talked about converting Shell to safety, but despite his reputation as an intelligent player, it seemed too difficult a task. Every NFL team passed on him in the 1974 draft.

Signed by Bill Nunn, Shell proved to be the find of the decade. He was the first guy on the field and the last guy off, and he ran, hit, and took instruction like a demon. When the dust settled, he made the team. Shell was relegated to special teams until safety Glen Edwards stepped aside in '77.

Shell was named to five Pro Bowls during a career (1974–87) that many think is worthy of Hall of Fame induction. His hits were of the bone-crushing variety, and his 51 interceptions are just six shy of Blount's team record.

"I always stayed in great condition," Shell explained of his prowess. "I only missed four games. It was a blessing."

The Turnpike Rivalry

Over the years, no Steelers rivalry has been as fierce and long-lived as the one with the Cleveland Browns—and for good reason. Connected by the Pennsylvania and Ohio turnpikes, the two cities are mirror images of one another. For more than a century, steel and coal were king in Pittsburgh and Cleveland, and each became known as a blue-collar, lunch-bucket town.

The Browns took a beating at Heinz Field on December 28, 2008 (pictured), when Pittsburgh held Cleveland to 20 passing yards in a 31–0 victory.

For decades, each team played in a cavernous antique—the Browns in Cleveland Municipal Stadium (1946–95) and the Steelers in Forbes Field and Pitt Stadium (1933–69). The Browns and Steelers boasted rowdy fans (from Pittsburgh's Franco's Italian Army to Cleveland's Dawg Pound), many of whom were ready to duke it out for the honor of their football team. The Pittsburgh faithful loved to pack their cars and drive to Cleveland (which they called "The Mistake by the Lake") for a game, a brew, and a brawl—whichever came first.

Having been beaten up pretty well by Jim Brown, Otto Graham, Lou "The Toe" Groza, and the rest of the Browns in the 1950s and '60s, the Steelers relished the turnabout in the '70s, when Pittsburgh regularly trounced the Brownies. One exception came in 1976, when Cleveland defensive end Joe "Turkey" Jones pulverized Terry Bradshaw, nearly breaking his neck while knocking him out for most of the season.

Rookie quarterback Mike Kruczek was called upon to play the next nine games. Hardly possessing Bradshaw's arm, Kruczek handed off. A lot. So much so that both Rocky Bleier and Franco Harris scampered to 1,000-yard seasons—the only time in Steelers history that two backs accomplished the feat.

The following season, Jack Lambert decked Browns quarterback Brian Sipe. Although the officials called it a late hit, the Steelers felt that justice had been served. Some of the old enmity dissipated when the Browns became the Ravens in 1996, but most of it returned in '99 with the new Browns, who played in the new Cleveland Browns Stadium.

The Turnpike Rivalry marches on. The two teams have played more than 100 games against each other over some 60 years, more or less breaking even, more or less despising each other.

Oh, is my eye disturbing your fist? Browns-Steelers games can get rough. In 1976, Turkey Jones nearly broke Terry Bradshaw's neck. The next year, Jack Lambert decked quarterback Brian Sipe. Here, Franco Harris takes one to the helmet in 1972.

PITTSBURGH STEELERS YESTERDAY & TODAY

The Lonely Thumb

Almost as soon as the Steelers won their fourth Super Bowl, T-shirts sprang up in Pittsburgh: "One for the Thumb in '81."

Sadly, it was not to be.

Dubbed the NFL's Team of the Decade for the 1970s, the Steelers simply ran out of steam. As former trainer Ralph Berlin put it, "Our guys got old. And they got old all at one time. It was somebody else's turn."

Drafting low throughout the winning years, the Steelers couldn't replenish their talent. Quarterback Mark Malone, receiver Weegie Thompson, and running back Frankie Pollard represented the team's mediocre roster. "When you draft last," said Chuck Noll, "you don't get the fertile minds you had before. We didn't have the great All-Pros."

After winning Super Bowl XIV, the Steelers went 9–7 in 1980 and missed the playoffs for the first time in nine years. The next year, they dropped to 8–8.

"Football can be very cruel," linebacker Jack Ham said. "Our defense in 1980–81 just wasn't good enough anymore. Plays we made before, we could no longer make."

In 1982 and '83, the Steelers bravely battled back, making the playoffs each year, but they were handily dispatched in the postseason. In 1985, Pittsburgh notched its first losing season in 14 years.

Still, the Steelers had their moments. Arguably, the best came in 1984 when the 9–7 Steelers beat the Broncos in the playoffs. Unfortunately, they faced red-hot Dan Marino and the Miami Dolphins the next week in the AFC title game. The University of Pittsburgh legend threw for 421 yards in a 45–28 rout.

"We had players who gave everything they had and more," Malone said. "But we didn't have the talent.... We were just another football team."

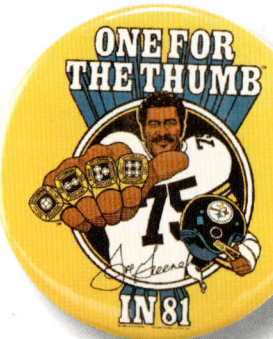

This "One for the Thumb in '81" button features a confident Joe Greene. Unfortunately, the team wasn't ready. In 1980–81, the Steelers finished out of the playoffs for the first time in nine years.

Mike Merriweather gets a bead on Denver quarterback John Elway in an AFC divisional playoff game in December 1984. Although the Steelers prevailed 24–17, it was Pittsburgh's only postseason win from 1980 to '88.

The Pittsburgh Maulers

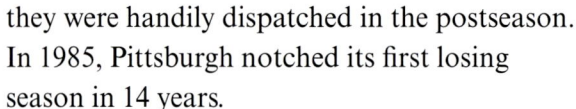

It was an idea whose time was mercifully brief. Spring football—that's what the upstart, 12-team United States Football League (USFL) tried in 1983. Despite losing money, the USFL added six teams in 1984, including the Pittsburgh Maulers.

With developer Edward J. DeBartolo backing them, the fledgling Maulers took the field in their purple and gray togs. Nebraska Heisman Trophy winner Mike Rozier and Pitt basketball star Sam Clancy were their gate attractions. Nevertheless, the Maulers finished 3–15 in 1984 while filling only about a third of Three Rivers Stadium.

With the league floundering, the USFL announced it would switch to the fall in 1986, which was unworkable in Pittsburgh. After the 1984 season, DeBartolo decided to fold the franchise. The entire league shut down after the 1985 campaign.

Stuck in Neutral

It was a long goodbye. In the 1970s, Chuck Noll had won four Super Bowls. But in his last seven years with the team, 1985 to '91, he was a sub-.500 coach.

"The great frustration," said former Steelers director of football operations Tom Donahoe, who joined the team in 1986, "was that we couldn't get any consistency. This was a great frustration for Chuck. Toward the end, he was tired of the whole process. He gave it a great effort, but this was wearing him out."

These were the dismal years—7–9 in 1985, 6–10 in '86, 8–7 in '87, and 5–11 in '88. Yet the maestro did have a last hurrah, engineering a great turnaround in 1989. Noll piloted the Steelers to a 9–7 finish and a trip to the playoffs.

Farewell to the Chief

It was August 1988, and shock waves rolled through Pittsburgh. Art Rooney Sr., the owner of the Pittsburgh Steelers since the team's inception in 1933, died at Mercy Hospital after suffering a stroke. He was 87.

With the city's flags at half-mast, and St. Peter's, his North Side church, standing room only, politicians and players, NFL brass, and family members said goodbye. Thousands more gathered outside the church as Pittsburgh paid homage to the most beloved man in its history.

Retired trainer Ralph Berlin could have been speaking for everyone when he said, "He was the finest man I've ever known. He was down to earth, sincere, and cared about people."

Making a point of learning people's names, the Chief had showed up at every Steelers practice. He personally brought coffee and sandwiches to the Three Rivers grounds crew when they had to spend all night changing the field from baseball to football.

"He never wanted you to be a big shot or anything special," his son Art Jr. recalled, "just a regular guy. He kept preaching that."

Steelers running back Merril Hoge shrugs off a Broncos tackler in the second round of the playoffs in January 1990. The Steelers' lone playoff team from 1985 to '91, this squad won the AFC wild card and then went west. Though the Steelers led Denver 23–17 in the fourth, a bad snap resulted in a 24–23 loss.

Pittsburgh featured quarterback Bubby Brister throwing from the shotgun, all-everything Rod Woodson scampering in the secondary, and Greg Lloyd punishing opponents at linebacker.

After defeating the Houston Oilers in the AFC wild card game 26–23, the Steelers steamed into Denver. Leading the Broncos 23–17 in the fourth quarter, all they had to do was manage the clock to get back to the AFC championship game. But a bad snap and a John Elway-led game-winning drive led to a painful 24–23 loss.

The Steelers went 9–7 in 1990 but didn't make the playoffs, and they stumbled to a 7–9 record in 1991. After 39 years in professional football and 209 wins (including playoffs) as Steelers coach, "it was time to go," Noll said. "No question about it."

Stars of the '80s

Tunch Ilkin was one of the frustrated Steelers of the 1980s—those who were drafted by the Team of the Decade only to find themselves playing on a Field of Futility.

"It was disappointing," he said. "When I came here [in 1980], I thought we'd get a Super Bowl. But my career coincided with the demise of the Steelers dynasty." Ilkin smiled ruefully. "I had this fear that the year I retired the Steelers would win another Super Bowl. There'd be a certain symmetry to that."

In the 1980s, he added, "we had a good football team—just not quite good enough. We didn't have that many great players."

The strongest and most durable Steeler of his time, center "Iron" Mike Webster started 150 consecutive games from 1975 to '86. The seven-time All-Pro was later diagnosed with brain damage and died in 2002 at the age of 50.

Certainly, the Steelers had steady, dependable players—a cadre of tough, durable professionals capable of big gains and bone-jarring hits. There were guts a'plenty, just very little glory.

Notables included:

Wide receiver **Louis Lipps**. Steeler Nation bellowed "Looooou" every time Lipps hauled in a pass. A two-time team MVP (1985 and '89), he possessed breakaway speed, hooking up with Bubby Brister on touchdown receptions of 80 and 89 yards in 1988. Lipps ranks among the team's career leaders in catches (358), reception yards (6,016), and touchdown receptions (39). As a punt returner, he set team records with 53 returns and 656 yards in 1984.

Center **Mike Webster**. Arriving in the Miracle Draft of '74, Webby anchored the offensive line through 1988. In the process, he set Steelers iron man records, including most

Louis Lipps made the Pro Bowl his first two seasons. After setting an NFL rookie record for punt return yardage in 1984 (656), he totaled 1,134 reception yards and 12 touchdown catches the next season as an All-Pro and team MVP.

THE STEELER DYNASTY: 1969–1991

From 1982 to '94, Gary Anderson set Steelers records with 309 field goals and 1,343 points. In 1983, he was voted team MVP after booming 27 field goals in 31 attempts. In 1993, he made 28 out of 30.

seasons (15), most games (220), and most consecutive games (177). Along the way, he set the gold standard for decency, sportsmanship, and excellence (nine Pro Bowl invitations).

Kicker **Gary Anderson**. Arriving in 1982, Anderson booted kicks for the Black and Gold for 13 seasons. He was a model of consistency, and 50-yard field goals were well within his reach. Team MVP in '83, he finished his Steelers career with 309 field goals and 1,343 points, both of which are team records. Anderson went on to play 23 seasons in the NFL and break the league's all-time scoring record.

Running back **Earnest Jackson**. Playing just three years with the Steelers (1986–88), Jackson rushed for more than 1,900 yards before retiring.

Offensive tackle **Tunch Ilkin**. A strong, intelligent player, Ilkin arrived in 1980 and played 176 games over 13 seasons.

Tackle and tight end **Larry Brown**. Like Webster, Brown was a holdover from the Super Bowl years. He arrived in 1971 and provided smart, steady blocking for 14 seasons. He caught 48 passes as a tight end, and he made the Pro Bowl as a tackle in 1982.

Cornerback **Dwayne Woodruff** (1979–85, 1987–90) snagged 37 career interceptions, including one that he returned 78 yards for a touchdown against Miami in 1988. He was the team's MVP in '82.

On defense, the Steelers always drafted well, notably the linebacker corps:

Bryan Hinkle (1982–93) delivered bone-shattering hits. He copped team MVP honors in 1986.

David Little, like Hinkle, was a durable hard-hitter. He played 179 games from 1981 to '92 and was the team's co-MVP (with Rod Woodson) in '88.

Robin Cole, an 11-year veteran (1977–87), had a nose for the ball, recovering 14 fumbles.

Mike Merriweather, arguably the valedictorian of the linebacker class, played just six years (1982–87) with the Steelers but was the definition of an impact player. He set a franchise record with 15 sacks in 1984. Merriweather, who earned team MVP honors in 1987, was named to three Pro Bowls.

Summing up the '80s, Louis Lipps said: "We always thought we could win. We always felt that we had the talent to put it all together."

But they never did.

Featured on this Topps card, Mike Merriweather set a Steelers record for sacks with 15 in 1984, including three in a game three times.

STEELERS MEMORIES

Quarterback, broadcaster, actor, country music star—Terry Bradshaw did it all. While certainly not a chart-topper, Bradshaw had enough fans to sell five albums, including 1981's *Here in My Heart*.

In one of the most famous sports commercials of all-time, a tired, beat-up Joe Greene tossed his jersey to a boy in return for a long, bottle-emptying swig of Coca-Cola. It played in print ads, too, as shown here.

In celebration of the Steelers' 50th season in 1982, fans selected the members of the All-Time Team. The dream squad included a pair of legendary hard-hitters, Ernie Stautner and Joe Greene.

Many Steelers cashed in on their notoriety—and why not? One of the most popular Steelers, Franco Harris, performed in commercials and endorsed a number of products, including Franco's Cheese Pizza.

Drafting low during the dynasty, the Steelers couldn't rebuild their team. The talent was good but not championship caliber. Here, a football (top and bottom are pictured) signed by players on the 1981 squad symbolized the end of an era.

Franco Harris is mobbed by fans at training camp in Latrobe, Pennsylvania, in 1982. Little did fans know that the ten-year veteran had another 1,000-yard season left in him.

According to *Inside Sports*, the Steelers would make a last stand in 1981. They still had plenty of fight, but they finished at 8-8 due to an 0-5 record in games decided by four points or fewer.

Jimmy Pol was a polka player par excellence. His memorable "Steelers Fight Song" and "Steeler Fever" were Pittsburgh best-sellers during the dynasty. Here, they're shown on 45-rpm records.

CHAPTER THREE

COWHER POWER
1992–2000

"You want emotion? Watch this football team play football for 60 minutes! We'll show you emotion!"

—ROOKIE HEAD COACH BILL COWHER, EXHORTING HIS TROOPS ON THE SIDELINES, 1992

Above: *In Bill Cowher's first six seasons as head coach (1992–97), the Steelers made the playoffs every year. They reached the AFC championship game three times and the Super Bowl once—for the first time in 16 years.* **Right:** *The best of Chuck Noll's holdovers and the cream of Bill Cowher's picks wound up in the Super Bowl in January 1996. Here, running back Bam Morris trots into the end zone for the Steelers' final touchdown in their 27–17 Super Bowl loss to Dallas.*

The Right Man for Pittsburgh

"Get us a good one," Dan Rooney told Steelers Director of Football Operations Tom Donahoe when Chuck Noll stepped down after the 1991 season. "A good person, with character and intelligence. A person who has the ability to teach and motivate the team."

That man was Bill Cowher, then a fresh-faced 34-year-old. Despite his youth, the Steelers' top brass liked what they saw. Cowher was passionate, intense, communicative. "He was very well organized," Donahoe recalled. "He had a plan for what he wanted to do, and could articulate that plan. He was also very enthusiastic, very consistent, and confident."

Born in Pittsburgh in 1957, Cowher starred in football, basketball, and track at Carlynton High. Although he wanted to play at Penn State, he ended up at North Carolina State. As a linebacker, Cowher was the Wolfpack's captain and MVP.

Graduating in 1979 with an education degree, he played for Cleveland (1980–82) and Philadelphia (1983–84). "I was always that guy who had to sweat out the 47-man roster to make the cut," he said. "As a marginal player, I had to find the way to succeed. So I spent the extra time studying, working, trying to find that little edge that would get me up to the gifted guy. That work ethic that I had to bring as a marginal athlete is one that I took over to coaching."

A protégé of Marty Schottenheimer, Cowher began his coaching career in 1985, at age 28, as the Cleveland Browns' special teams coach. He became the team's secondary coach before following Schottenheimer to Kansas City in 1989 as defensive coordinator.

Three years later, he was the Steelers' head coach. "Change is very difficult for everybody," safety Carnell Lake said, "especially if you're comfortable and making progress. But coach Cowher came in very motivated, very personable, and that helped alleviate any anxieties that I had at the time. I wondered, 'Is he going to come in and slash and burn, or is he going to come in and see what kind of talent he has here?' He came and saw—and instilled a greater sense of team unity."

As one example, Cowher invited Lake into his office to express "my wishes and desires about where this team might be headed," Lake said. "In three years, I never once [had been] in coach Noll's office. It was a totally different setting and environment—and a very comfortable one. I felt I could express my individuality, yet be a part of a team concept of winning. We were able to sit down as coaches and players and go over a game plan. Everyone had input, so everyone felt like they were part of something special."

"Coach Cowher inherited a team that had a lot of talent," cornerback Rod Woodson added, "and he molded that talent

The most visibly emotional coach in Steelers history, Bill Cowher consistently inspired his team to greater achievements. Here he hugs quarterback Neil O'Donnell after defeating Indianapolis in the AFC championship game in January 1996.

> "I WAS ALWAYS THAT GUY WHO HAD TO SWEAT OUT THE 47-MAN ROSTER TO MAKE THE CUT."
>
> — BILL COWHER, ON HIS NFL PLAYING CAREER

into his own team. Everybody says he's a player's coach, because he talks to players and has an open line of communication. He also respects every player on the football team and gives each one an opportunity to prove himself—even if they do wrong. He gives them a lot of respect, and they play a lot harder for themselves and the team."

For his part, Cowher knew what he was getting. "I wasn't coming to a team that didn't have good players or didn't know how to win," he said. "I was very fortunate to

As distant as Chuck Noll could be from his players, Bill Cowher was just the opposite. One standard Cowher practice was the postgame prayer, as shown here after their 34–17 win over the Broncos in the AFC championship game in January 2006.

follow coach Noll, for he left a great work ethic on the football team."

Planning, evaluating, and cutting judiciously, Cowher recreated the team, passed more often, and constructed "Blitzburgh"—a faster, more aggressive defense. "He made the system fit the players," Woodson said, "instead of making the players fit the system. When coach Cowher did that, he provided the opportunity for the players to blossom."

No one ever accused Chuck Noll of being soft, but workouts were tighter and practices more intense under Cowher. "It's an organization attempt to win a championship," Cowher preached. "We're all in this thing together. That's the bottom line. We win as one, and we lose as one."

The immediate result: an 11–5 rookie record in his first season—the team's best record since 1979—and Associated Press and *Sporting News* Coach of the Year honors.

"There was no doubt that he was going to fit in," Dan Rooney said. "He was almost an extension of Noll."

More than most NFL coaches, Cowher could get heated on the sidelines. Numerous NFL officials got an earful from the vociferous Steelers coach.

Building a Contender

Even though the Steelers hadn't been to the playoffs since 1989, Chuck Noll left his successor, Bill Cowher, a rich crop of talent. "It wasn't like the cupboard was bare," said former Steelers director of football operations Tom Donahoe. "Maybe some of the guys needed to hear a different voice. Maybe they needed a different direction."

Upon taking the reins in 1992, Cowher inherited such blue-chippers as cornerback Rod Woodson, safety Carnell Lake, linebacker Greg Lloyd, center Dermontti Dawson, and quarterback Neil O'Donnell—the core of the Super Bowl XXX team.

Cowher drafted massive offensive linemen, such as 300-pounder Leon Searcy in 1992. With the quarterback protected, Cowher used O'Donnell to best advantage. There would be no Bradshaw-esque long balls, which QB Bubby Brister had tried. Instead, the new scheme called for flares and screens, low-risk plays that netted high completion rates.

The Steelers employed a corps of solid receivers. Ernie Mills, Andre Hastings, Yancey Thigpen, and Charles Johnson could be counted on for a few hundred yards apiece each season. Dan Rooney called them "the best group of receivers we've ever had—as a group." The Steelers further improved the offense by making third-year man Barry Foster the No. 1 running back in 1992, the year he rushed for 1,690 yards.

From 1992 to '94, Cowher led the Steelers to the playoffs every year with records of 11–5, 9–7, and 12–4. In two of those seasons, they finished second in the NFL in fewest points allowed. Unfortunately, Pittsburgh lost in the first round to Buffalo in 1992 and Kansas City in 1993. Then, after trouncing Cleveland 29–9 in a 1994 divisional playoff game, the Steelers lost the AFC title game at home to San Diego 17–13. Two 43-yard Stan Humphries touchdown passes in the second half did them in.

Nevertheless, the Steelers were poised to make a Super Bowl run in 1995.

Barry Foster rushed for 3,252 yards from 1992 to '94, but he couldn't lead the Steelers past the Chargers in the January 1995 AFC championship game.

Foster's Big Year

Drafted 128th overall by Chuck Noll in 1990, 5'10", 220-pound power back Barry Foster came into his own under Bill Cowher. Plowing out of the backfield, Foster in 1992 set multiple Steelers rushing records, including 390 carries, 12 100-yard games, and a Steelers-record 1,690 yards, second most in the NFL that year. Against the Jets, he amassed 190 yards on 33 carries.

Injured on and off for the next two seasons, Foster never again achieved greatness. After five years with the club (1990–94), he signed with Carolina and Cincinnati but played for neither team, retiring at age 26. His 62 games and 3,943 rushing yards with the Steelers remain his entire NFL record.

"I'm proud that I was a part of that Steelers era," Foster said. "I thought I would end my career as a Steeler. It's one of the biggest regrets I have."

Cowher Power: 1992–2000

A Super Bowl Quarterback

It began with much promise—the man with the golden arm putting up glittering numbers across the board.

A third-round pick out of Maryland in 1990, the 6'3", 228-pound Neil O'Donnell spent his first year watching. As a sophomore in 1991, he shared the starter's role with Bubby Brister.

Liking O'Donnell's poise, strength, and durability, rookie head coach Bill Cowher hired Ron Erhardt in 1992 to design an offense around his wunderkind. In addition, Cowher created a mammoth offensive line behind which O'Donnell could hide for weeks at a time: Leon Searcy (300 pounds), Dermontti Dawson (286), John Jackson (293), Todd Kalis (296), and Justin "Jugs" Strzelczyk, the Steelers' behemoth banjo picker (291).

Immediately, Cowher's hunch paid off. In his last four years with the club (1992–95), O'Donnell led the Steelers expertly. He took the team to the playoffs every year while putting up outstanding passing numbers, including the lowest interception rate in club history.

In 1992, his 59.1 percent completion rate set a team record. In 1993, O'Donnell's best year, he set team records with 486 attempts and 270 completions, good for 3,208 yards—a mark that only Bradshaw had eclipsed among Steelers quarterbacks. In Cincinnati on September 19, 1993, O'Donnell completed 21 of 25 passes for an 84 percent rate, then the highest for a single game in Steelers history.

In the Super Bowl season of 1995, the year his teammates voted him Most Valuable Player, O'Donnell's 59.13 percent completion rate and four 300-yard passing games set single-season Steelers records. He also established single-game team marks for attempts (55) and completions (34).

Though O'Donnell seemed poised for the pantheon, the normally surgically precise quarterback threw two interceptions to Cowboys cornerback Larry Brown in Super Bowl XXX. The errant throws cost him the game and, ultimately, his career in Pittsburgh.

O'Donnell bore the brunt of the fans' ire during the 27–17 loss. A free agent after the season, he took a $25 million offer from the Jets, $7 million more than the Steelers' best offer. O'Donnell, who went 39–22 as Pittsburgh's field general, departed with a number of team records, all since eclipsed. His career team marks included a 57.1 percent completion rate, 81.6 passer rating, and five 300-yard games. As a Steeler, O'Donnell passed for 12,867 yards and 68 touchdowns.

Fellow Steelers QB Bubby Brister bid him a fitting farewell. "Neil was a great quarterback," Brister said. "He played well. He led the team."

He did it all. Except win a Super Bowl.

A quintessential pocket passer, Neil O'Donnell set bushels of Steelers throwing marks—many of which have been surpassed. Yet his greatest triumph was also his greatest defeat. After leading his team to Super Bowl XXX, his three interceptions lost the game.

PITTSBURGH STEELERS YESTERDAY & TODAY

Woodson Makes an Impact

Is there an ultimate Rod Woodson moment? Probably not, for the Hall of Fame cornerback, safety, and punt and kick returner had far too many to list.

But here's one:

It was September 8, 1996, Three Rivers Stadium. Having missed nearly the entire 1995 season with a torn ACL, he had miraculously returned to play in Super Bowl XXX. Still, as the '96 campaign opened, there were questions about Woodson—and the team.

The first game confirmed fans' fears. After the Steelers lost the opener in Jacksonville, along with four linebackers, everyone wondered about the season. With the Ravens coming to Pittsburgh, what would the Steelers, and Woodson, do? He did what impact players do—step up. On Baltimore's second play of the game, Ravens quarterback Vinny Testaverde tested Woodson. He answered by intercepting the pass and running it back 43 yards for a score. The Steelers never looked back, steaming to the division championship.

"When you come to play the Pittsburgh Steelers," Woodson said, "you're going to remember it."

An electrifying player, the 6'0", 200-pounder out of Purdue was the Steelers' first-round draft choice in 1987. Over his 17 NFL seasons, the first 10 with the Steelers, Woodson's impact was so extraordinary that he made the Hall of Fame in his first year of eligibility in 2009.

Earning 11 Pro Bowl berths, a record for a defensive back, Woodson was a six-time All-Pro selection at cornerback and safety. Woodson holds the NFL record for career touchdowns from interceptions with 12. He finished with 4,894 kickoff return yards and 2,362 punt return yards, and he returned four kicks for touchdowns. He played in three Super Bowls for three teams: Steelers, Ravens, and Raiders. The 1993 NFL Defensive Player of the Year, Woodson stands third all-time with 71 interceptions, returned for a record 1,483 yards.

A three-time Steelers MVP, Woodson amassed 38 interceptions to rank fourth in team history. He is second in all-time interception return yards (779), and his five interception returns for touchdowns are a team record. He also remains the team's career leader in punt return yards (2,362) and kickoff return yards (4,894).

Said Woodson: "I like the challenge of playing defense. 'You know where you're going. I don't. Let's play.'"

"I enjoy the game," he added. "I've dedicated myself to it—studying film, understanding offenses, getting a feel for it. Then letting go."

A defensive back, kick returner, and punt returner, Rod Woodson was a three-time Steelers MVP (1988, '90, and '93). As an All-Pro in 1993, he made 95 tackles and picked off eight passes while logging a career-high 42 punt returns.

> "WHEN YOU COME TO PLAY THE PITTSBURGH STEELERS, YOU'RE GOING TO REMEMBER IT."
>
> ROD WOODSON

COWHER POWER: 1992–2000

Double Yoi!

Yoi and *double yoi, okel dokle* and *um-hah,* and dozens more, all emanating from a little man with a big voice—a voice, one man once wrote, that sounded like a garbage disposal grinding up a root beer bottle.

Born Myron Kopelman, Myron Cope was the rare bird who got to play both sides of the table—the lovable, spluttering clown and the credible, hard-working reporter. Most broadcasters have trouble enough with one; Cope excelled at both.

A trained newspaperman who once shared the *Sports Illustrated* masthead with George Plimpton, he gave radio commentaries, worked a talk show, and, most memorably, shared the Steelers broadcast booth.

Arriving in 1970, when the team moved to Three Rivers Stadium, Cope was a throwback to a time when announcers were less corporate and more colorful. Still, insiders knew Cope as one of the best, most dedicated professionals in the broadcasting business. "Nobody worked harder," said retired Steelers public relations director Joe Gordon. "Nobody cared more. He had high standards and great creativity."

By the end of 2004, it was time to say goodbye. At halftime on Halloween Night, 2005, a sold-out Heinz Field stood and cheered as Cope was presented his own black 35 jersey for his 35 years of service. "Myron," Dan Rooney said, "always made it fun for everyone."

"I came along totally by accident," said Cope, "and then I was the color analyst for a team that had gone nowhere for years. All of a sudden you've got a dynasty being born. I was just a guy along for the ride."

"I think I was able to establish a great degree of credibility with listeners," he added. "I shot straight—and did my research."

Steeler Nation mourned his loss on February 27, 2008, when he died at age 79.

Myron Cope was a hard-working reporter who brought a rich sense of the absurd to every broadcast. In 2005, he won the Pro Football Hall of Fame's Pete Rozelle Radio-Television Award.

Cope's Nicknames

Cope spiced up his broadcasts with colorful, original nicknames—not just for players, but for teams, too.

On the field, there were the "Bungles" (Cincinnati), "Cleve Brownies," and "Mini Vikes." As for players, "when I decide a guy is ripe for one," Cope said, "I try to come up with something that has reason and originality." For example, he called Jack Lambert "Jack Splat" "because the guy hit and splattered people," Cope said. "I played off that nursery rhyme Jack Spratt—he's a tall guy, too."

Or "Emperor Chaz" for Chuck Noll. "Every dynasty has to have an emperor," Cope explained. (Predictably, Noll hated it.)

Then there was Jack "The Hydroplane" Deloplaine—but anyone could have come up with that.

PITTSBURGH STEELERS YESTERDAY & TODAY

To the Super Bowl, Baby!

The night before Super Bowl XXX, Steelers linebacker Jerry Olsavsky got on the team bus. "This is it, baby," he thought.

And he knew all his teammates were feeling the same thing.

Nothing speaks more loudly about Bill Cowher's coaching and leadership skills than the 1995 season. In his fourth year as head coach, Cowher—who at 38 became the youngest-ever Super Bowl coach—kept the team focused. "We had the talent," center Dermontti Dawson recalled. "We knew if everyone did what they were capable of, we could do something. That's what happened."

In the January 1996 AFC championship game, only one touchdown was scored in the first three quarters—a five-yard pass from Neil O'Donnell to Kordell Stewart. Entering the final quarter, the Steelers led the Colts 13–9.

The '95 team combined the best of both Steelers worlds. First, there was Chuck Noll's predilection for quickness, strength, and agility—perfect for Blitzburgh. Then there was Cowher's insistence on sheer bulk on the offensive line, which gave Neil O'Donnell or Kordell Stewart time to throw and the running backs the chance to chew up yardage and the clock.

The Steelers featured a fearsome 3–4 defense. Brentson Buckner, Joel Steed, and Ray Seals manned the line, while Kevin Greene, Levon Kirkland, Chad Brown, and Greg Lloyd comprised a world-class linebacking corps. With Carnell Lake, Willie Williams, Darren Perry, and Myron Bell in the secondary, opposing quarterbacks didn't stand much of a chance.

With an offensive line held together by Dawson, O'Donnell taking the snaps, Erric Pegram and Bam Morris running the ball, and a solid corps of wide receivers including Yancey Thigpen and Ernie Mills, the Steelers were formidable offensively, too.

Nevertheless, 1995 hardly began as a championship season. On Opening Day at Three Rivers Stadium, the scoring consisted of two short Bam Morris touchdown runs and three Norm Johnson field goals, as Pittsburgh nipped the Lions 23–20. The Steelers looked better the next week at the Astrodome. Andre Hastings returned a punt 72 yards for a touchdown. Tight end Mark Bruener took in a 15-yard TD pass. Johnson kicked two field goals. And Carnell Lake returned an interception 32 yards for a touchdown. The Steelers won 34–17.

Pittsburgh entered the 1995–96 playoffs at 11–5, thanks to an eight-game winning streak late in the season. With 409 yards of offense, they crushed Buffalo 40–21 in their first playoff game (pictured). Here, receiver Ernie Mills makes one of his patented circus catches.

COWHER POWER: 1992–2000

But in Miami against Dan Marino's Dolphins, everything seemed to unravel. The Steelers coughed it up five times—three interceptions and two fumbles—as Miami triumphed 23–10. The miscues continued the next week, as five straight turnovers (seven overall) gave the game to the Vikings, 44–24. A 31–16 Three Rivers victory over the Chargers was just the thing to get the Steelers back on track.

Or not. With a 20–16 loss to the Jaguars in Jacksonville and a 27–9 home loss to the Bengals, the Steelers were 3–4. "It was tough in the beginning of the year," Levon Kirkland said, as quoted in the *Pittsburgh Post-Gazette*. "We were really scrambling at the time. We were really lost at the time and didn't have a whole lot of answers."

That's when Cowher stepped up, announcing that the new season would begin immediately. It would last just nine games, and the intensity would be off the charts.

Out for revenge against Jacksonville, the Steelers breezed 24–7, with Thigpen, Pegram, and fullback John Williams all scoring before the Jaguars got on the board. The next week, the Black and Gold did something they had been unable to do 11 straight times—beat the Bears in Chicago. With the score seesawing back and forth, Ernie Mills tied it with a fourth-quarter touchdown reception. In overtime, a Johnson field goal subdued the Bears 37–34.

The next week, the Steelers cow-kicked the visiting Browns 20–3, with O'Donnell and Stewart connecting with Thigpen

Trailing 16–13 in the fourth quarter of the AFC championship game, Pittsburgh's Bam Morris ran in the game-winner. On the game's final play, shown here, Indianapolis receiver Aaron Bailey (80) dropped Colts quarterback Jim Harbaugh's Hail Mary pass in the end zone.

"The Ultimate Warrior"

The numbers only partially explain how Carnell Lake made the NFL All-Decade Team for the 1990s. In a ten-year Steelers career (1989–98), Lake recovered 16 fumbles, running two back for touchdowns. In 1997, he led Pittsburgh in sacks—the only time a cornerback has done that. During his NFL career, which included time in Baltimore and Jacksonville, Lake played in five Pro Bowls, four as a Steeler.

"The ultimate warrior," receiver Ernie Mills said. "Big, strong, fast—the best strong safety in the game."

"Carnell," former lineman Tunch Ilkin added, "would just *tag* you."

Drafted in the second round as a UCLA linebacker, Lake was converted to safety. In 1995, when Rod Woodson was injured, Lake took over at cornerback. The result: a Super Bowl for the team and another Pro Bowl for Lake.

Lake's all-time Steelers highlight came on October 19, 1997, at Riverfront Stadium. After the Bengals' Carl Pickens caught a Jeff Blake pass on his own 45, then motored unimpeded toward pay dirt, Lake raced after him, caught Pickens on the Steelers' 15, and whacked the ball out of his hands.

"He was one tough dude," said former defensive back Jack Butler. "He played it 100 percent."

A triumphant Bill Cowher hoists his first AFC championship trophy. Inheriting a team that had gone 7–9 in 1991, Cowher infused the Steelers with a new kind of fire. He capped four consecutive playoff seasons with a trip to Super Bowl XXX.

and Mills. Revenge was even sweeter against the Bengals, with Pittsburgh pummeling Cincinnati 49–31. Pittsburgh put up 21 unanswered points in the fourth quarter, highlighted by a 71-yard touchdown pass from O'Donnell to Stewart.

In Cleveland, Pittsburgh won a squeaker 20–17 on a 27-yard Johnson field goal. After crushing Houston 21–7, the Steelers put a hurt on the hated Raiders in Oakland. Mills scored twice and Norm Johnson booted five field goals as Pittsburgh prevailed 29–10.

Back home against New England, Thigpen and Mills caught TD passes, Stewart ran one in, and Chris Oldham ran back a Greg Lloyd-induced fumble for a 41–27 win. Having won eight straight, the Steelers dropped the season finale to Green Bay 24–19.

Champions of the AFC Central, the 11–5 Steelers hosted the Bills in the AFC divisional playoff game. Shuffling all over Buffalo, Mills caught five passes, including one for a touchdown. Morris ran for 106 yards, and Jerry Olsavsky, Cornell Lake, and Levon Kirkland picked off passes. The Steelers prevailed 40–21.

Hosting the Colts in the AFC championship game, Pittsburgh and Indy traded field goals until Stewart took a five-yard O'Donnell pass for a score. The Colts moved ahead in the fourth quarter on a 47-yard pass play, but the Steelers would not be denied. O'Donnell led a last-ditch drive that culminated when Morris scored from one yard out with just over a minute remaining to give the Steelers a 20–16 victory.

"Turning around a 3–4 record and going to a Super Bowl," Dermontti Dawson recalled, "was a dream season. All the coaches, including coach Cowher, were always positive. Always kept hope alive. Never dwelled on the negatives."

With the drawing power of the Steelers and especially the Cowboys—who had won Super Bowls to cap off the 1992 and

In the fourth quarter of Super Bowl XXX, Pittsburgh trailed the Cowbowys 20–7. But after a Norm Johnson field goal, a successful onside kick, and this Bam Morris touchdown run, the score was 20–17. The Steelers had a chance.

'93 seasons—Super Bowl XXX would attract 94.1 million viewers, making it the most-watched sporting event in history at that time.

> "ALL THE COACHES, INCLUDING COACH COWHER, WERE ALWAYS POSITIVE. ALWAYS KEPT HOPE ALIVE. NEVER DWELLED ON THE NEGATIVES. THAT WAS A BIG FACTOR."
>
> STEELERS CENTER DERMONTTI DAWSON

Dallas, behind stars Troy Aikman and Emmitt Smith, drew first blood, then continued to strike. With Dallas up 13–0, the Steelers overcame a third-and-19 and, later in the drive, scored on a six-yard pass from O'Donnell to Yancey Thigpen.

The Cowboys led 20–7, but the Steelers cut it to 20–10 on a 46-yard Johnson field goal with 11:20 remaining. After surprising Dallas with a successful onside kick, the Steelers used short passes to move the ball to the 1-yard line, from which

Dallas defensive back "Neon" Deion Sanders breaks up a pass to Yancey Thigpen. Although the Steelers outgained the Cowboys (310–254) and had more first downs (25–15), Dallas had zero turnovers and Pittsburgh three—all interceptions.

With the score 20–17 Dallas in the fourth quarter, and the Steelers still very much alive, Cowboys cornerback Larry Brown picked off his second Neil O'Donnell pass (pictured). The Cowboys went on to score, making the final 27–17.

Morris ran it in. Unfortunately for Pittsburgh, O'Donnell was intercepted for the second time by game MVP Larry Brown. Smith scored to clinch the victory, 27–17.

"Going to the Super Bowl was very special," Carnell Lake recalled. "The team concept that Bill Cowher preached came through for us. We overcame a lot of shortcomings and disadvantages to wind up there."

"It was a great experience," Cowher agreed. "I don't like losing any games. But I was very proud of our football team, especially the way they responded after being down early. That was indicative of our 1995 season. We played 60 minutes of football, and we fought until the very end. They had every reason to walk out with their heads held high."

STEELERS MEMORIES

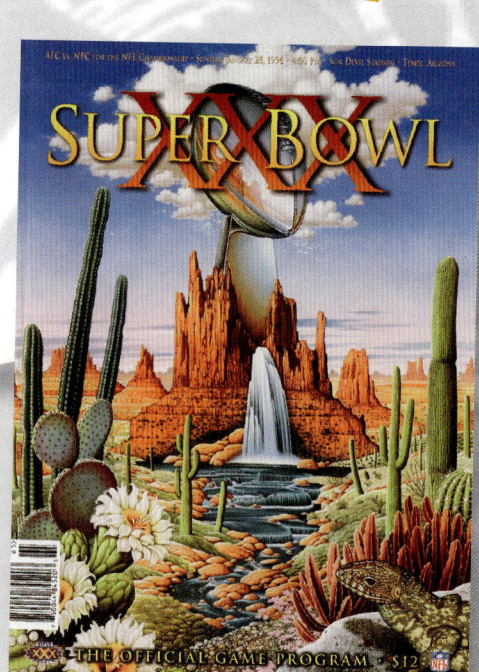

In 1994, the 12-4 Steelers looked like they could go all the way. But in the AFC championship game, they squandered a 10-3 halftime lead and lost a heartbreaker to the Chargers 17-13.

The Steelers played in Super Bowl XXX in arid Arizona. Neil O'Donnell had the lowest interception rate in team history, but his errant passes cost Pittsburgh the title.

Having lost two Super Bowls to the '70s Steelers, the Cowboys were gunning for Pittsburgh in Super Bowl XXX. When the dust settled, Dallas stood tall, but Wheaties commemorated both teams.

Who cares if it's silly as long as it's the Steelers? With America's most loyal fans, the Steelers enjoy unmatched road attendance—represented by this trio at Super Bowl XXX.

Rarely has a Steeler inspired fans in such a short period of time. Sack machine Kevin Greene, honored with this Starting Lineup action figure, came in 1993 and left after Super Bowl XXX.

Although Bill Cowher never displayed such musculature, his distinctive chin is accurate on this button. A popular coach during his Steelers tenure, he inspired buttons, T-shirts, and banners.

Linebacker Greg Lloyd, featured on *Street & Smith's Pro Football Guide*, was a 240-pounder with a black belt in Tae Kwon Do. His bone-jarring hits thrilled Steelers fans and inspired his teammates.

Neil O'Donnell was the Steelers' "Knight Raider," as depicted on this Coca-Cola Monsters of the Gridiron card. But the loss of Super Bowl XXX cost him the fans' loyalty.

In Pittsburgh, defense is the name of the game. This pigskin is signed by a quintet of All-Pro defensive players—Mel Blount, Jack Ham, Andy Russell, Jack Lambert, and Rod Woodson.

PITTSBURGH STEELERS YESTERDAY & TODAY

Almost Heaven in '96, '97

The sweat had hardly dried from Super Bowl XXX when Neil O'Donnell, Leon Searcy, and Kevin Greene departed for greener pastures. "Those were big losses," Carnell Lake said. "Those guys left voids."

"Whatever holes are created by free agency," Tom Donahoe added, "you have to figure out a way to plug them."

Plug they did. Employing both Mike Tomczak and Kordell Stewart at quarterback, and letting new acquisition Jerome Bettis run wild, the Steelers went 10–6 in 1996.

In their second game, fueled by a Rod Woodson interception against the Ravens, the Steelers coasted to a 31–17 victory. Not to be outdone, Carnell Lake picked off a pass against the Bills the next week and raced in for a score, sparking the Steelers to a 24–6 victory.

Emerging as the NFL's most exciting and most versatile quarterback—a scrambler and 60-yard passer—Stewart busted off an 80-yard touchdown run in the season finale against Carolina. It was the longest by a quarterback in NFL history.

In the playoffs against the Colts, Woodson literally threw a blocker into the running back, knocking them both down on the way to a 42–14 win. In the infamous "Fog Bowl" in Foxboro, the Patriots stunned the Steelers 28–3.

In 1997, Stewart led the way to an 11–5 finish. In a game at Baltimore, he helped the Steelers overcome a 21-point deficit. He threw for three touchdowns and ran in two to pull off a thrilling 42–34 victory. Stewart became the first NFL quarterback to throw for 20 touchdowns and run for 10 in a season.

After beating the Pats in the playoffs (7–6 on a Stewart 40-yard run), the Steelers fell to the Broncos in the AFC championship game. They trailed 24–14 at the half and lost 24–21. It was the start of a three-year tailspin.

The Steelers beat the Colts 42–14 in a December 1996 wild card game but lost the next week at New England 28–3. In foggy conditions, Steelers quarterbacks amassed only 110 passing yards on 39 throws. Here, the Patriots' Terry Glenn burns Rod Woodson for a reception.

The American Bowl

With the 1997 American Bowl, Dan Rooney furthered Irish economic development—and Irish peace.

Rooney's Newry/Pittsburgh Partnership hosted a business affair in Dublin, and Dan brought the Steelers with him. In Dublin's 82,000-seat Croke Park, the Steelers beat the Chicago Bears 30–17 on July 27. They also were feted by the lord mayor of Dublin, U.S. Ambassador Jean Kennedy-Smith, and the Royal Dublin Society.

As part of his continuing mission, Rooney said: "We embraced Protestants and Catholics, Irish Republicans, and British Loyalists. We spoke at cities all over America, raising awareness about peace and reconciliation, rejecting the politics of violence, and raising funds for causes like integrated schools between Catholics and Protestants."

Along the way, Dubliners got to appreciate American football—Steelers style.

COWHER POWER: 1992–2000

Here Comes "The Bus"

The first bright spot of the Steelers' 1996 season came on Draft Day, when Pittsburgh practically stole three-year veteran Jerome Bettis from the St. Louis Rams. Even though the power back out of Notre Dame had averaged 1,030 yards a season with the Rams, they felt he no longer fit in their system, so they dealt Bettis and a third-round choice to Pittsburgh for second- and fourth-round picks.

They called Bettis "The Bus" because he was built like one (5'10", 250). "I've never been shy about eating," he said. "They don't call me The Bus because I pass the plate." From 1996 to 2005, Bettis gave the Steelers their first great runner since Franco Harris. He won multiple team MVP honors, led the Steelers to a Super Bowl victory, and retired with 13,662 yards rushing, which placed him fifth in NFL history.

"Jerome epitomized what Pittsburgh is all about," Tunch Ilkin said. "This town loves tough guys. Jerome is a bona fide tough guy."

"Coming to the Steelers was a dream come true," Bettis said. "This was a team just off the Super Bowl—a winning organization, a talented group of guys. But the biggest part was that I was coming to a place that appreciated big running backs even more than quarterbacks. That helped, because I *loved* to play."

Bettis was quick and agile enough to slice through holes, but mostly he motored straight ahead like a black and yellow school bus. Bettis would break one tackle, then another, until a swarm of defensive backs drove him to the ground.

"I tried to be physical in running the football," Bettis explained. "I tried to inflict punishment on the defenders instead of just taking it. When I did that, I got defenders to turn away. After getting hit so many times, their mentality changed from being aggressive to just trying to get me on the ground. Then they had to play my game. I was able to make them miss me, or bounce off them and keep going."

Overall, Bettis's numbers are staggering. He tallied ten 100-yard games in both 1996 and '97, and he amassed 1,665 yards in 1997. He lugged the ball 375 times that year, including 36 carries (and three touchdowns) at Arizona.

Setting the all-time Steelers mark with 50 100-yard games, Bettis finished second to Harris in virtually every other rushing category, including 10,571 yards rushing, 2,683 carries, and 78 rushing touchdowns. "Jerome was an inspiration," Bill Cowher said, "a great leader."

> "I'VE NEVER BEEN SHY ABOUT EATING. THEY DON'T CALL ME THE BUS BECAUSE I PASS THE PLATE."
>
> — JEROME BETTIS

One of history's greatest power backs, Jerome Bettis broke tackles, extended drives, and gained all-important short yards. Bringing a new level of leadership to the Steelers, he powered the Black and Gold to six playoff berths in ten seasons.

World's Greatest Fans

"It's practically unheard of," Myron Cope commented, "to find a fellow who's left Pittsburgh and has adopted another city's football team. They're Steelers fans for life."

"The fans are a special part of Steelers history," agreed former Steelers director of football operations Tom Donahoe. "They're passionate. They want to win, and they want to go to the Super Bowl every year. But they never give up on the team. Their loyalty and consistency are remarkable. It never ceases to amaze me that when we play a road game how many Steelers fans come to the hotel and to the game."

"Our fans are passionate," Donahoe continued. "They *love* football. As long as we give them a constant effort, and play a physical brand of football, they can live with the results. Having said that, the fans almost don't let us lose. They've been a huge part of our success. They're not something we ever take lightly."

Nor should they. With more than 300 straight sellouts—dating back to November 5, 1972, including regular season and playoffs—and a *six-year* season-ticket waiting list, the Steelers have the No. 1 fans in America, according to ESPN. As Matt Mosley wrote: "Steelers fans are deserving of the top honor. The decline of the steel industry in the 1970s coincided with the rise of the Steelers dynasty. At a time when the city's collective psyche was taking a major blow, the local football team offered a weekly respite. A generation of young people left the city to find work elsewhere, but they remained passion-

Freezing cold, blizzards, even ice storms—nothing stops Steelers fans from cheering the Black and Gold. Decked out in team gear—watch caps, scarves, jackets, hand warmers, you name it—Steelers fans are everywhere on Game Day, from Heinz Field to halftime neighborhood pickup games.

Steeler Nation

They are uncounted and uncountable, the global members of the Steeler Nation. With as many as 1,500 coast-to-coast bars and restaurants identifying themselves as Steelers-related, fans can hoist a flag in every state—and find fellow travelers from England to Australia, Israel to Egypt, Italy to Ecuador.

"You go into sports bars in any city on game day," observed *USA Today*'s Gary Mihoces. "There are six Bills fans. There are six Browns fans. And there are 300 Steeler fans. In every city. It's unbelievable."

They are road warriors, as well. It is not uncommon, for example, to have 30,000 very vocal Steelers fans attending a Giants-Steelers game in New Jersey.

"We take pride in our roots as Pittsburghers," said Vince Laschied III, who moved to Los Angeles some 40 years ago. Added scholastic football coach T. J. Troup, from Tustin, California, "The Steelers are resilient, passionate, fight-to-the-end warriors—like Pittsburgh itself!"

ate about their hometown team. And that's why your local stadiums are often invaded by a black-and-gold army."

Of course, the fans are expected to make life miserable for visiting teams at Heinz Field—but on the road? That fact impressed former player Ross Tucker. After an estimated 25 percent of the fans in Jacksonville waved Terrible Towels, Tucker wrote in *Sports Illustrated* that the Steelers had the most dominant fan base in the NFL. By consistently traveling to road games to support their team, Steelers fans give their club an advantage that no other NFL club could match.

"The simple truth," Tucker added, "is very evident to every player in the NFL: Steelers fans are the best in the business."

The Steeler Nation's road-game presence makes a big impact. Normally a home team feeds off the fans' emotions, but when there's a large number of fans cheering the *other* team, it puts a crimp in the home team's emotional reserves. Second, the hometown noise that ruins counts and audibles doesn't work as well when a large portion of the fans are not hollering.

The theory is supported by statistics. From 1996 through the 2005 campaign, the Steelers had the best road winning percentage in the NFL in regular-season play (.550), even though their overall winning percentage was only fourth best (.616). "Seemingly, no stadium is truly immune to the Steelers culture," Tucker wrote.

Don't think it isn't appreciated. At the AFC Victory Party at Heinz Field on January 18, 2009, head coach Mike Tomlin told the fans, "I absolutely love you guys!"

The feeling is mutual.

Once a pea coat crowd in the 1940s and '50s, Steelers fans now dress in player jerseys, paint their faces, and wave their Terrible Towels. Around the holidays, a number of Santa Clauses head to Heinz Field—including this one in a Bettis jersey.

With packed stadiums beginning in 1972, and no end in sight, the Steelers boast the best fans in sports, according to ESPN. So many fans travel with the team that even road games seem like they're at home—as at Super Bowl XLIII (pictured).

Butting Heads with the Bengals

Perhaps it's because coaches Chuck Noll and Sam Wyche descended from Paul Brown, making it a kind of sibling rivalry. (Noll famously refused to shake Wyche's hand after Bengals games.) Perhaps it's because Bill Cowher and Marvin Lewis are old friends—and old adversaries.

Or perhaps it's because Pittsburgh and Cincinnati share a common river, the Ohio, and always seem to be squaring off against each other. During the 1970s, for example, the Pirates and Reds met in the National League playoffs four times in ten years, with both teams winning the World Series twice during that decade.

For pure venom and world-class trashtalking, brutal hits and bone-crushing blocks, nothing beats the annual home-and-away Steelers-Bengals series. Playing Pittsburgh twice a year since 1970, when Cincinnati joined the league, the

Called "The Nastiest Rivalry in the NFL" by *Sports Illustrated*, Bengals-Steelers games always seem to be marked by brutal hits and trash talk. Despite the Steelers' dominance since 1970, the Bengals won both match-ups in 2009—ensuring enmity in the ensuing years.

Bengals—whom the Steeler Nation derisively calls the "Bungles"—seem to save their greatest hatred for the Black and Gold.

Perhaps it hearkens back to the Steelers' dynasty days, when, on a safety blitz, Pittsburgh's Mike Wagner nearly severed quarterback Kenny Anderson's spine with a pile-driver tackle. Perhaps it's about the 1998 season, when the Bengals went 3–13 but beat the Steelers twice.

"Every time they play us," Steelers running back Willie Parker told the Associated Press, "they play their 'A' ballgame. Every time we play them, it's tough."

Nevertheless, Pittsburgh has won roughly 60 percent of its games against Cincinnati, including a 1992 contest in which the Steelers shut out the Bengals 22–0, recording ten sacks of rookie quarterback David Klingler.

The rivalry went into overdrive during a playoff victory in the Queen City in 2005. Pittsburgh's Kimo von Oelhoffen injured Bengals QB Carson Palmer's knee, knocking him out of the game. The Steelers went on to win 31–17 en route to the world title. Palmer had surgery and extensive rehab.

To add insult to injury, after the game Steelers coach Bill Cowher led a "Who Dey? We Dey" chant, mocking a Bengals tradition. "Cincinnati," Hines Ward said, as quoted in the *Pittsburgh Post-Gazette,* "is our home away from home."

Pumped up over that, Bengals wide receiver T. J. Houshmandzadeh wiped his shoes with a Terrible Towel—a desecration if ever there was one.

There's no love lost between AFC North rivals Pittsburgh and Cincinnati. Here, wide receiver T. J. Houshmandzadeh—the same Houshmandzadeh who once wiped his feet with a Terrible Towel—stiff-arms safety Troy Polamalu.

Blown Calls

We all know about Mel Blount, his devastating midfield hits, and the rule change about hitting open receivers. But he wasn't the only Steeler to force a rule change. There was also Jerome Bettis, who starred in—as Sherlock Holmes might have called it—The Case of the Curious Coin Toss.

On Thanksgiving Day, 1998, The Bus returned home to Detroit. With the Steelers and Lions tied 16–16, the game went to overtime. During the coin toss, Bettis called tails. Referee Phil Luckett said the Steelers called heads. It landed on tails.

Bettis was clearly stunned, but he could do nothing about it. The ball went to the Lions, who drove downfield, kicked a field goal, and beat the Steelers 19–16. ESPN would vote Luckett's blunder as the seventh worst blown call in the history of sports.

At it turned out, the Steelers never recovered, losing their next four games to finish at 7–9.

That's when the NFL changed the rule, ensuring that the call must be made before the coin is tossed—and that at least two officials be there to hear it.

The Steelers finished 6–10 in 1999, but that season still wasn't as frustrating as 2000. That was the year that the Steelers may have set a record for losses due largely to blown calls, with three. Against Cleveland, Tennessee, and Phila-

Pittsburgh's Wayne Gandy (72) is ejected on January 2, 2000, for pushing a referee. During the game, Titans backup quarterback Neil O'Donnell defeated the Steelers 47–36. The following year, a bad call cost Pittsburgh a timeout that could have reversed a 23–20 Tennessee victory.

Kent Graham is sacked by the Browns on September 17, 2000. Extra time taken off the clock cost the Steelers a chance for a tying field goal.

delphia, calls went against the Steelers that clearly contributed to the team's losses and its mediocre 9–7 record.

Against Cleveland, the referees botched the final seconds of the clock so badly that the Steelers lost a precious five seconds—time that kept Pittsburgh from kicking a tying field goal. The result: 23–20 Browns. Against Philadelphia, the Eagles recovered an onside kick, drove, kicked a field goal, and won in overtime 26–23—even though the Eagles committed an uncalled penalty during the onside kick.

Perhaps the most egregious call of all came against Tennessee, when Hines Ward caught a third-quarter Kent Graham pass and scored. Or did he? After officials ruled Ward down at the 1-yard line, Cowher tossed the red flag. Call upheld; timeout lost. The Steelers scored on the next play, but they nevertheless lost a precious timeout, which they could have used in the 23–20 loss.

When the NFL admitted its mistake, that Ward had indeed crossed the goal line, a seething Bill Cowher told reporters, "It should have been a touchdown. That's great to know."

PITTSBURGH STEELERS YESTERDAY & TODAY

They Called Him Slash

He came with a can't-miss tag, a second-round pick out of the University of Colorado with more pure talent than anyone had ever seen. Kordell Stewart could pass, run, catch, and even kick—he could do it all.

And then he couldn't.

Arriving in 1995, Stewart as a rookie made 30 first downs—14 rushing, 13 receiving, 3 passing—and scored on a 71-yard reception. They called him "Slash" after the keyboard symbol—for quarterback/wide receiver/running back/punter. The nickname became so ubiquitous that even Bill Cowher used it.

Stewart, though, didn't like it. "I'm capable of doing a lot of things," he said at the time, "but I'm a quarterback. That Slash thing, that's fine and dandy. But I'm Kordell Stewart, and I'm a quarterback."

By season's end in 1996, Stewart was emerging as a true NFL star. A year later, he threw for 3,020 yards and 21 touchdowns and ran for 476 yards, leading the Steelers to the AFC championship game.

Then came the hard times, 1998 to 2000, with Stewart under-throwing and underachieving and Pittsburgh missing the playoffs each year.

> "THAT SLASH THING, THAT'S FINE AND DANDY. BUT I'M KORDELL STEWART, AND I'M A QUARTERBACK."
>
> KORDELL STEWART

Gifted with more physical talent than any quarterback in Pittsburgh history, Kordell Stewart twice topped the 3,000-yard passing mark. What he couldn't do was win the big game, failing in the 1997 and 2001 AFC championship games.

In 2001, for a brief, shining season, Stewart played like the No. 10 of old. Voted team MVP, he set a career high in passing yards (3,109) and was named to the Pro Bowl. Against the Ravens, Stewart threw for a career-best 333 yards. Again he led the Steelers to the AFC title game, but they lost to New England 24–17, with Stewart throwing a costly interception.

In 2002, after the Steelers opened at 1–3, Stewart was benched in favor of Arena Football League veteran Tommy Maddox. Slash was gone after the season. He played just 12 games with Chicago and Baltimore before hanging up his helmet/pads/cleats for good.

In eight years with Pittsburgh, Stewart had passed for 13,328 yards and 70 touchdowns, both of which ranked second in Steelers history at the time. Nevertheless, his career passer rating was a mediocre 72.3.

Everyone asked what happened.

"When you're a great athlete, you rely on your athleticism," Tunch Ilkin commented. "If you're blessed with too much ability, sometimes you don't grow in other areas. You don't develop the intangibles, the mental part of your game."

"To this day I don't think Kordell gets the credit he should," Art Rooney II said. "If you look at Kordell's record, he was a winning quarterback for us. It's an unfortunate chapter in Steelers history that he didn't get recognized for the good things. Bottom line: he got us to the AFC championship game twice."

Rivaling with the Ravens

"Pure hatred," Hines Ward said with an evil grin. That's the same Hines Ward who in 1998 belted Steeler-turned-Raven Rod Woodson hard enough to bloody his nose. In 2007, Ward decked Ed Reed so badly that former Steelers (on hand for ceremonies honoring the team's 75th anniversary) winced on the sidelines.

Never forgiving, never forgetting, Ravens linebacker Terrell Suggs in 2008 said "the bounty was out on Hines." (Suggs, investigated by the NFL, said he was only joking. Some joke.)

Steelers-Ravens. It's a rivalry that goes from motormouth to smashmouth and back again. Some say it's a vestige of the pre-1996 days, when the Ravens were the Cleveland Browns, and the Pittsburgh-Cleveland rivalry was as intense as it got in the NFL. In those more pugilistic times, it was not uncommon for out-of-state cars to have their tires slashed—and for so many fights to break out in the stands that Pittsburghers called old Cleveland Muni the Punch Palace.

After the Browns moved to Baltimore, the two franchises picked up where they had left off, but added cayenne pepper to the mix. They then set the pot to boiling after the 2002 realignment, when the Steelers and Ravens annually fought for supremacy in the AFC North.

First, the war of words.

"His time will come," Ravens linebacker Bart Scott told the *Pittsburgh Post-Gazette* about Ward before the 2008 AFC championship game. Scott asserted that one day, some player would take out Ward's knee. "The guy will be fined and [Ward] will be gone," Scott said. "No one will care. No one will send him any cards saying they're sorry. Not to that guy. You reap what you sow."

"I take pride in trying to get up under their skins," Ward said. "I guess they're trying to knock the smile off my face."

Sometimes it's more than smiles that get knocked off. Consider the Ryan Clark bone-crusher that sent Raven Willis McGahee to the hospital in 2008. Or the Ray Lewis fracture of Steelers rookie Rashard Mendenhall's shoulder during the same season.

There have been lesser infractions, such as the 2002 incident that got Pittsburgh's Plaxico (whom the Ravens' Shannon Sharpe had called Plexiglass) Burress and Baltimore's James Trapp tossed for fighting.

"The coaches hate each other," Ward told the press, "the players hate each other. There's no calling each other after the game and inviting each other out to dinner. The feeling's mutual: They don't like us, and we don't like them. [When we play,] it's going to be one of those black and blue games."

The Steelers-Ravens rivalry has burned since the birds were the Browns and nobody could stop Jim Brown. Since 1996, when the franchise moved to Baltimore, no games have been harder hitting. Here, a bareheaded Kelly Gregg tries to put a big hurt on Big Ben.

Stars of the '90s

No, they didn't win a Super Bowl, but the 1990s Steelers featured an enormous collection of talent. There were dismal years at the end of the decade, when it seemed that the team couldn't even win the coin toss. But by and large, the Cowher years at Three Rivers Stadium, 1992 to 2000, spelled success. The Steelers went to the playoffs six of those nine seasons, including a trip to Super Bowl XXX.

Such success was based on the stellar efforts of a group of first-rate players—the best of the Noll holdovers and the choice Cowher-era acquisitions. The offense featured Kordell Stewart, Jerome Bettis, and a corps of sure-handed receivers. The aptly titled "Blitzburgh" defense boasted Rod Woodson, Carnell Lake, and a group so rough and rowdy that 1970s Steelers linebacker Andy Russell said, "I'm impressed with their superb athleticism and their great talent. They're stronger, bigger, faster than we were. They would beat us."

The players Bill Cowher justifiably called the "60-Minute Men" included, on offense:

Center **Dermontti Dawson**. One of

Soft-spoken off the field and a monster on it, center Dermontti Dawson snapped the ball like a concert violinist—and blocked like the Rock of Gibraltar. Here, he lines up in front of the symbol for Jerome Bettis—a yellow school bus.

Durable, with breakaway speed, wide receiver Yancey Thigpen set Steelers records for receptions and receiving yards—1,398 in 1997 alone. Here, he races by the Bengals' Greg Myers on the way to a 20–3 Steelers victory in 1997.

Chuck Noll's last great draft picks, man-mountain Dawson arrived in 1988, played through 2000, and continued the line of great Steelers centers, following Ray Mansfield and Mike Webster. Playing 181 games over 13 seasons, 170 consecutively (second most ever by a Steeler, behind Webster), Dawson earned seven straight Pro Bowl invitations (1992–98) and made the NFL All-Decade Team for the '90s. "I studied game plans," he said. "I wanted to make sure I knew everything."

Wide receiver **Yancey Thigpen**. Coming from the Chargers in 1992 and staying through '97, Thigpen possessed jackrabbit speed, Houdini-like moves, and hands like a vice. Emerging as the Steelers' primary receiver in 1995, he proved his mettle by setting the team's single-season reception record with 85. Two years later, he set the team record for reception yards in a season with 1,398.

And on the other side of the ball:

Linebacker **Levon Kirkland**. No one had ever seen anyone like Levon Kirkland, a lynchpin on the Steelers defense from 1992 to 2000. At 6'1" and playing between 275 to 300 pounds, he had the bulk of a defensive tackle yet scampered like a safety. He seemed to be all over the field all at once, making seemingly impossible plays.

Kirkland led the 1996 Steelers with 113 tackles to go along with four interceptions and four sacks. Yet his numbers simply cannot reflect his enormous value to the club. A first-team All-Pro in 1997, he was named to the NFL All-Decade Team for the '90s.

Linebacker **Greg Lloyd**. Hard-driving, fiery, and a fan favorite, Lloyd duly earned a spot on Pittsburgh's 75th Anniversary Team. A Steeler from 1988 to '97, he was perhaps the hardest hitter of the decade, smashing anything that moved. A 225-pound outside linebacker, Lloyd ranks among the Steelers' all-time leaders in sacks with 53.5. "It's almost as if Greg has turned off the switch and is running on pure emotion," Carnell Lake said at the time. "We feed off Greg."

"He's just ruthless," Barry Foster added admiringly, "and about as tough as they come."

Linebacker **Kevin Greene**. A Steeler for only three seasons (1993–95), Greene was nevertheless a true impact player, racking up 35.5 sacks and earning a berth on the NFL All-Decade Team. After logging 12.5 sacks his first year with Pittsburgh, Greene led the NFL in sacks in 1994 with 14 and earned his second straight Pro Bowl invitation in 1995.

Linebacker **Jason Gildon**. The all-time Steelers sackmeister with 77, Gildon, who played from 1994 to 2003, was a one-man wrecking crew in 2000, notching 13.5 sacks, 77 tackles, and one defensive touchdown.

Bill Cowher said about the 1990s Steelers: "We like to get players who have produced. But we also like to get players that we can feel comfortable with when adversity strikes, when you go through the bad times, the guys who want to rally around you and respond to you. Rod Woodson, Greg Lloyd, Carnell Lake, Dermontti Dawson, and Yancey Thigpen—these are the guys you're looking for. They understand the team commitment. They understand what teamwork is all about and are willing to make the sacrifices that go along with being successful."

After rebuilding when he came, Cowher would rebuild again in 2001. And a decade after losing his first Super Bowl, he would find, in 2005, the right cast of characters to win his second.

When it came to coverage—and sheer physical strength—no Steeler in the 1990s could match linebacker Levon Kirkland. Averaging nearly 100 tackles per year as a Steeler, No. 99 seemed to cover the entire field all by himself.

As a strong safety and cornerback, Carnell Lake wreaked havoc all over the field. He recovered six fumbles as a rookie in 1989 and was named to five Pro Bowls (four as a Steeler).

STEELERS MEMORIES

Fiery Bill Cowher and multi-talented Kordell Stewart, pictured on the cover of TV Guide, made for good television in the late 1990s and early 2000s.

As part of the U.S. Postal Service's "Celebrate the Century" series, the four-time Super Bowl champs were honored in 1999 with a postage stamp featuring a Steelers helmet in Three Rivers Stadium.

Hot Rod indeed! Over ten seasons, no Steeler electrified the fans more than No. 26, Rod Woodson, whose killer hits and breakaway moves often made the difference in close games.

The Steelers reached new heights of popularity in the '90s. Led by new coach Bill Cowher, himself a Pittsburgh native, the new, exciting Steelers rekindled fans' interest in the Black and Gold.

Along with its Heinz Field series, Rolling Rock issued a four-can set commemorating Myron Cope's four decades with the Steelers.

Kordell Stewart became a fan favorite during his first season as a regular starter, 1997, when he threw for 3,020 yards and ran for 476—with 32 total touchdowns.

The 1990s bobblehead craze hardly escaped the Steelers. No. 92, linebacker Jason Gildon, was prized for his grit, determination, solid service, and team-record 77 sacks.

No player symbolized the hard-driving, win-at-all-costs Steelers as much as running back Jerome Bettis. People paid any price to share a piece of his fame, as indicated by this signed jersey.

CHAPTER FOUR

HIGH TIMES AT HEINZ FIELD
2001–Today

"Steelers football is never going to be pretty. Throw style points out the window. These guys will fight to the end. We didn't blink."

—**HEAD COACH MIKE TOMLIN, AFTER WINNING SUPER BOWL XLIII**

Above: *In the new century, the Steelers hit pay dirt twice, winning both Super Bowl XL, under Bill Cowher, and Super Bowl XLIII, under Mike Tomlin.* **Right:** *Fast Willie burns 'em again! Against San Diego in an AFC divisional playoff game in January 2009, running back Willie Parker scores a second-half touchdown to put the game out of reach.*

PITTSBURGH STEELERS YESTERDAY & TODAY

A Home of Their Own

With the Pirates hectoring for a new ballpark through most of the 1990s, Pittsburgh and Pennsylvania finally came through with enough money to make the baseball club's investment worthwhile. While that was happening, the Steelers similarly negotiated for a new home.

> "IF THE PIRATES GOT A NEW PLACE, WE WERE NOT GOING TO STAY AT THE OLD PLACE. WHAT WE GOT WAS HEINZ FIELD, WHICH IS ONE OF THE GREAT THINGS IN THIS CITY."
>
> — DAN ROONEY

"Three Rivers was 30 years old," Dan Rooney said, "and our position was we would stay there if the Pirates did. But if the Pirates got a new place, we were not going to stay at the old place. What we got was Heinz Field, which is one of the great things in this city. The Pitt Panthers play here, and the high schools, too. We wanted Heinz Field for everyone."

And it is. Opening in 2001, two years after its groundbreaking, the Steelers' new home was the work of many people, most notably Art Rooney II. The corporate attorney had been schooled to take over the franchise, just like *his* father, Dan, had been groomed by his father to run the team. Heinz Field, Dan said, "was Art's biggest feat. He worked with the political people, in Pittsburgh and Harrisburg."

He also worked with lending institutions. "We incurred a significant amount of debt to make Heinz Field happen," Art II said. "Historically, we never had any debt. My

As shown on the cover of the 2001 Steelers media guide, Heinz Field opens onto Pittsburgh's Point. Heinz Field is also home to the University of Pittsburgh Panthers, and it hosts many high school championship games.

For the first time in their history, the Steelers didn't have to share a stadium with the Pittsburgh Pirates. Opening in 2001, the 65,000-seat, $300 million, football-only Heinz Field replaced 30-year-old Three Rivers Stadium.

grandfather didn't believe in borrowing money. Most of the time he ran the organization out of his pocket."

Aside from Heinz Field, the Steelers also added new offices and an extensive multifield practice facility at the South Side UPMC Sports Performance Complex, which they share with the Pitt Panthers.

At the "Mustard Palace," as it's affectionately known for its association with Heinz and its 65,000 yellow seats, the Rooneys deliberately kept the number of seats low so that the field would open onto Pittsburgh's Point—with its Three Rivers and majestic fountain. At nearly 1.5 million total square feet, Heinz Field cost nearly $281 million, with $8 million for the Jumbotron and its control room. The H. J. Heinz Company agreed to pay $57 million over 20 years to have the field named after the company.

Composed of 12,000 tons of structural steel, 7 miles of handrail, 238,000 bolts, 48,000 cubic yards of concrete, and 8 million pounds of sand, Heinz Field stands 150 feet high, with a scoreboard nearly 100 feet long. The famous twin red-zone ketchup bottles, which shift and pour when the Steelers are within the 20, are 35 feet long and weigh 4 tons each.

Heinz Field is the quasi-official home of regional high school championship games. In fact, more than 60 high schools have won City League or WPIAL titles at Heinz, contributing celebratory murals to the stadium's interior walls.

The 40,000-square-foot Coca-Cola Great Hall, a fan favorite, contains numerous attractions, including Super Bowl trophy replicas. Ten murals portray the history of the Steelers and Western Pennsylvania football. And a Steelers Hall of Fame, with Three Rivers Stadium lockers, lionizes such luminaries as Andy Russell, Rocky Bleier, Jack Lambert, and Dwight White.

At the center of it, Heinz Field boasts a two-acre bluegrass playing field, with 35 miles of underground tubing that keeps the sod at 62 degrees.

Many have commented on the oft-chewed-up turf, but former Steelers player and coach Dick Hoak shrugs off such criticism. "People complain that Heinz Field is dug up," he said with a shrug. "But that's part of football. It's grass. If it wears out, it wears out, and you go play."

Spoken like a true Steeler.

Heinz Field is located on Pittsburgh's North Side, across the Allegheny River from downtown's Golden Triangle. It is a short walk from the Carnegie Science Center, National Aviary, and Andy Warhol Museum. It is also across the river from Pittsburgh's Cultural District, with its shops, restaurants, and theaters.

Bradshaw Returns

He had led the Steelers through the dynasty from 1970 to '83, but despite four Super Bowl rings and enshrinement in the Pro Football Hall of Fame, Terry Bradshaw fought his private demons—including the Pittsburgh fans.

He said bad things. He stayed away. Fear gnawed at him. He endured clinical depression so pervasive that it busted three marriages and prevented his return to his adopted city. When he did agree to come to Heinz Field,

nearly 20 years after retirement, Bradshaw's fear was so great that he brought his two teenaged daughters, Rachel and Erin. *They'll never boo me with the girls there,* he figured.

Finally, he walked onto the field at halftime on October 21, 2002, to have his No. 12 retired by the club. That's when 63,000 people rose as one, cheering, applauding, waving their Terrible Towels.

Standing at the 50-yard, drinking in the ovation, he said, "That sounds good. You keep going." Then he hugged his daughters. "I've missed you all terribly much," he told the crowd. "It's good to be home. Thank you. God bless all of you."

Three INTs Short of a Super Bowl

It began as a very good year, one of the best. As the Steelers opened Heinz Field in 2001, Jerome Bettis rushed for 153 yards, putting him over the 10,000-yard mark for his career. (The Bus would finish the season with his sixth straight 1,000-yard campaign.)

Then, with the team 3–1, Bettis showed off his rifle arm, throwing a touchdown pass to tight end Jerame Tuman against Tampa Bay. "I'll do whatever we have to do to score," he said. (He also ran for 143 yards.) Sacking the Bucs QB ten times, the Steelers won 17–10.

Pittsburgh improved to 5–1 until the Ravens upset the apple cart, 13–10, with the Steelers missing four field goals. At Tennessee, both Kordell Stewart and Amos Zereoue played scatback, running for touchdowns in a 34–24 win. Over one stretch, the Steelers won seven straight games to improve to 12–2. They finished at 13–3.

In the playoffs, Pittsburgh shot down the Ravens at Heinz Field 27–10. The next week, the Steelers were heavily favored against New England in the AFC championship game. But once again, Stewart couldn't win the big one. He threw three interceptions, including two in the last three minutes, to cement the Steelers' 24–17 defeat.

For the Steelers, it was three of four AFC championship game losses under Bill Cowher, all at home, all with the Black and Gold favored.

Cowher came under fire for each loss, of course, but for Stewart, who also threw three interceptions in the January 1998 AFC championship game loss to the Broncos, it was one defeat too many. More than anyone, the multitalented quarterback bore the brunt of the fans' ire—perhaps with good reason.

"He seemed to have the physical talent," Chuck Noll observed, "but I'm not sure he wanted to do everything that you have to do to be a winner. A lot of time that's sacrificing your own ego. I don't know that he was willing to do that."

"I am still a big Kordell fan," Hines Ward countered. "He had three different offensive coordinators in three years. He lost [receivers] Yancey Thigpen and Charles Johnson. Then he was asked to lead the younger guys. It put a lot of pressure on him."

Despite the disappointing ending, the Steelers had ended their three-year rut. Throughout the rest of the decade, the team would begin almost every season as a legitimate Super Bowl contender.

Amos Zereoue dives into the end zone against Baltimore in an AFC divisional playoff game in January 2002. Riding high, the 13–3 Steelers went on to drub the visiting Ravens 27–10, holding Baltimore to just 150 total yards.

Against the Patriots in the January 2002 AFC championship game, Kordell Stewart threw three interceptions, including two in the last three minutes to doom the Steelers to a 24–17 defeat. Here, defensive back Myron Bell consoles him late in the game.

HIGH TIMES AT HEINZ FIELD: 2001–TODAY

Tommy Gun Gets It Done in 2002

Tennessee tried to send Pittsburgh to the AFC championship game in January 2003, but the Steelers couldn't capitalize in overtime after two blown Titans field goals.

But first things first.

After the Steelers started the 2002 season 0–2, Bill Cowher replaced quarterback Kordell Stewart with Arena Football League veteran Tommy Maddox. Overnight, he became "Tommy Gun," a pocket passer who found receivers all over the field.

Pittsburgh's Deshea Townsend breaks up a pass in a January 2003 AFC wild card game against the Browns. The Steelers scored 22 points in the fourth quarter, on two Tommy Maddox touchdown passes and a Chris Fuamatu-Ma'afala TD run, for a 36–33 win.

"It's one of those strange cases in the NFL," Art Rooney II said, "a matter of being in the right place at the right time and getting the right opportunity.... In 2001, we were looking for a backup quarterback and weren't expecting a lot out of this guy. But he impressed everybody in his first training camp. After that, no one was shocked that he came in and played so well in '02."

A man who went ten years between NFL starts, Maddox had been Denver's first-round pick in 1992. Traded, released, picked up, released, and then out of the NFL for five years, Maddox still kept sharp. "[I] worked out with my old high school, just in case the call came," he said.

It did in 2000, from Arena football. Maddox played for the New Jersey Red Dogs, which led to an invitation to the Steelers camp the following year. "Quarterbacks are hard to move around," Maddox said. "You have to know the guys, know the system. Here, the system fit me well. The guys made me feel at home."

With Tommy gunning 'em, and Hines Ward and Plaxico Burress catching everything in sight, the Steelers amassed 5,952 yards in 2002—fifth most in the NFL—and finished 10–5–1. As AFC North champions, they faced the Browns at Heinz Field in a wild card game. The Black and Gold trailed by ten points entering the fourth quarter before erupting for 22 points. The result: Steelers 36–33, with Maddox throwing for 367 yards and three touchdowns.

Against the Titans on the road, Pittsburgh again trailed in the fourth quarter but came back, taking a 31–28 lead before Tennessee tied it. At that point, Titans kicker Joe Nedney's last-second, 48-yard field goal attempt could have been the game-winner. It wasn't. In overtime, Nedney got another chance—and blew it.

But with the play wiped out due to a controversial running-into-the kicker penalty, Nedney got another opportunity and came through, splitting the uprights from 26 yards out.

The pain of that loss wasn't as bad as the entire 2003 season. The Steelers finished last in the NFL in '03 with 3.3 yards per rush and finished at 6–10. What happened the next season shocked the nation.

Former Arena Football League quarterback Tommy Maddox set numerous Steelers records in 2002, including most passing yards in a game (473 against the Falcons).

PITTSBURGH STEELERS YESTERDAY & TODAY

The Go-To Guy

He owns them all now. Hines Ward tops the charts for all of the major Steelers receiving categories. Through the 2009 season, he had amassed 895 receptions, 10,947 receiving yards, and 78 touchdown catches. The only Steeler to come close to his 112 receptions in a season (2002) is himself, with 95 in '03 and 94 in '01. Moreover, his streak of consecutive games making a reception extends more than a decade.

Not bad for a 1998 third-round draft pick out of Georgia (No. 92 overall) who had to fight his way off special teams.

"Whoever would've thought that a guy who played special teams—a flyer, a gunner—would become the all-time reception leader?" Ward asked. "It means so much for me personally, considering everything I've been through—being a third-round pick, overcoming two first-rounders drafted in front of me, playing on a predominantly run-oriented team, having all the naysayers say I'm not tall, I'm not fast. I kept working hard, but I never thought of breaking the record."

Despite his modest athleticism, the four-time Pro Bowler (2001–04) became one the Steelers' big-play guys—whether or not he had the ball.

"I'm not the flashiest guy," Ward said. "I just want to be the guy the quarterback can count on to do whatever it takes to catch the ball. I've been through five quarterbacks since I've come here, and I've had to adjust to them all. I've worked extra hard to do that. They all trusted me to make the plays, and that's what I try to do."

Around the NFL, Ward is known as a nasty combatant. "He's the toughest wide receiver I've ever seen," Steelers broadcaster Myron Cope said. "He looks for people to hit."

"Hines goes down with some of the great Pittsburgh Steelers," Bill Cowher commented. "He's caught a lot of passes here, and no one appreciated it more than I did. Not just his catching, but what he brings to the game. He's the complete football player. He plays with a lot of passion."

"It's a big honor to wear this uniform," Ward said. "Especially with all the great players who were here before me and how important the Steelers are to the city of Pittsburgh. This city is very passionate about its football—and I understand that."

> "HE'S THE TOUGHEST WIDE RECEIVER I'VE EVER SEEN. HE LOOKS FOR PEOPLE TO HIT."
>
> MYRON COPE, ON HINES WARD

As Seoul City Mayor Lee Myung-bak consoles him, Hines Ward, the first half-Korean NFL superstar, weeps at Seoul City Hall after his successful Super Bowl XL exploits. A Seoul native, Ward has worked tirelessly to help biracial Korean children.

The toughest wide receiver in Steelers history, Hines Ward worked his way up from special teams to Super Bowl XL MVP. Owner of virtually every Steelers receiving record, Ward catches everything in reach—while doling out killer blocks for his teammates.

15-1 with a Rookie QB

When he arrived in Pittsburgh, Ben Roethlisberger was a 22-year-old quarterback, a former beanpole wideout grown large—6'5", 240 pounds. While starring at Miami of Ohio, the tough, smart field general had thrown a school-record 84 touchdown passes—impressive enough to net him first-round NFL Draft status in 2004.

As a Steelers rookie, he backed up Tommy Maddox. The 2004 season started with a win against the Raiders. But in the second game, against Baltimore, Maddox was badly injured, and the Steelers had to bring in the rookie. Roethlisberger completed 12 of 20 passes for 176 yards and two touchdowns, but the Ravens won 30–13.

It would be the Steelers' only loss of the regular season.

In hurricane-soaked Miami, they beached the Dolphins 13–3. They proceeded to roll over the hapless Bengals 28–17, whip the Browns 34–23, and outgun the Cowboys 24–20, with Roethlisberger orchestrating a come-from-behind win. "While he has a good supporting cast around him that enables him to perform quickly," Chuck Noll said, "he looks like a veteran."

Against the Patriots, in the seventh game, Big Ben came out smoking. The Steelers took a 24–3 lead over the defending Super Bowl champs and prevailed 34–20. The Eagles flew into town—and crawled home. Down 16–14 against the Jaguars, Ben marched 'em downfield to set up the winning Jeff Reed field goal.

Against the Jets and Giants, Pittsburgh came up with big plays that won ballgames. After beating Buffalo, the Steelers became the fourth NFL team in history to go 15–1. They were also the first to win 14 straight on a 16-game card, including 13 by a rookie quarterback.

"Sure, we were surprised," Bill Cowher said. "We didn't expect what took place because it's never been done before."

In the postseason against the Jets, Roethlisberger threw two interceptions, one for an 86-yard touchdown return, but the Black and Gold won in overtime 20–17. Facing the Patriots in the AFC championship game, Roethlisberger threw three interceptions, including an 87-yard TD return. Final: 41–27 New England.

"We didn't expect him to do what he did," Art Rooney II recalled. "We had high hopes for him, of course, but as a player for the future. He's one of those guys who makes people around him better, not only by the things he can do physically—he obviously has great talent—but also by his approach as a winner.

"Walking on the field, he makes people believe they can win games."

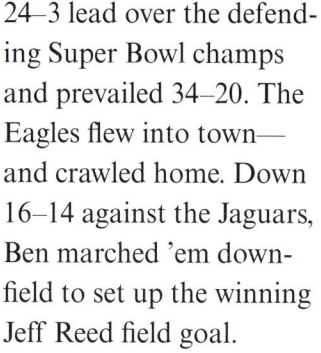

In 2004, rookie Ben Roethlisberger stepped in for the injured Tommy Maddox and led Pittsburgh to a 15–1 season.

Jeff Reed nails a game-winning field goal against the Jets in an AFC divisional playoff game in January 2005. The thrilling 20–17 overtime victory was Pittsburgh's 15th win in a row.

STEELERS MEMORIES

Never have a few lengthy locks inspired so much commotion. Wearing his hair in traditional Polynesian style, Troy Polamalu has inspired much chatter—and many wigs worn to Steelers games.

Antwaan Randle El lined up as a wide receiver, kick returner, and punt returner. But the former college quarterback could also throw—which helped the Steelers win Super Bowl XL.

The H. J. Heinz Company not only made its mark on Heinz Field with giant ketchup bottles, but it also produced regular-sized, commemorative ketchup bottles honoring Heinz Field and the Steelers' 2005 championship season.

In 2007, in honor of the team's 75th anniversary, the Steelers introduced their first and only mascot, Steely McBeam. The name, submitted by fan Diane Roles, was chosen from 70,000 entries.

A statue of Steelers founder and eternal spirit Art Rooney sits outside Heinz Field, welcoming all comers. The Chief remains the most beloved figure in Pittsburgh history.

The Steelers were 16-1 and had won 15 straight games when they hosted the AFC championship game in January 2005. Pittsburgh fans were sure the Steelers were going to the Super Bowl—until New England raced to a 24-3 halftime lead.

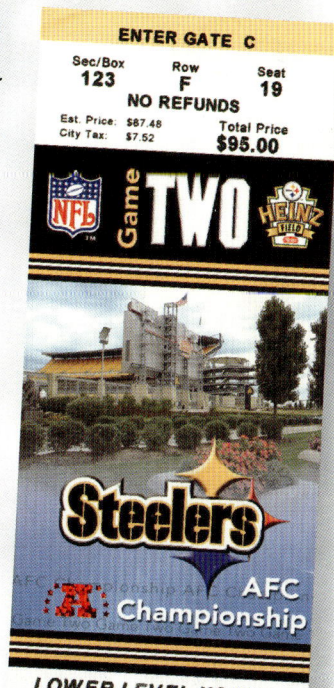

Nothing adorns a Steelers fan's desk better than a signed miniature helmet from Joey Porter, a true fan favorite for both his freewheeling speech and his bone-jarring hits.

From selling insurance in Texas to selling out stadiums in Pittsburgh, Tommy Maddox became an overnight sensation, inspiring T-shirts, banners, and even his own brand of barbeque sauce.

PITTSBURGH STEELERS YESTERDAY & TODAY

High Five!

It was 2005, Big Ben's sophomore year. The Steelers were still charged up about their 15–1 campaign in 2004, but they were still smarting over the loss to New England in the AFC championship game.

Would that gut-wrenching experience strengthen their young quarterback—and anneal the team's wounds? Or would it send the Steelers into a season-long funk? In training camp, everyone could see the changes in Roethlisberger. He was not the hesitant, tentative quarterback from the 2004 playoffs, the one who had thrown five interceptions in two games. This Ben took his time, managed the offense, and inspired his team.

"The difference is experience," Bill Cowher said. "He's been there. He does a good job being the leader."

During a summery season opener at Heinz Field, Roethlisberger passed for two touchdowns and running back Willie Parker rushed for 161 yards against Tennessee. (He'd finish the season with 1,202.) The final: Steelers 34, Titans 7.

Despite 100-degree heat at Reliant Stadium, Ben and the boys scored on their first four drives against the Texans. The Big Nasty D sacked David Carr eight times, and Pittsburgh won 27–7. The following week, the Steelers nearly avenged their loss in the 2004 AFC championship game, but New England kicked a field goal with one second left to break a 20–all tie.

"We'll bounce back from it," Cowher said. "We have to."

Against the Chargers, the Steelers trailed 22–21 late in the game. With six seconds left, Jeff Reed kicked a 40-yard field goal for a 24–22 victory. With Roethlisberger banged up, Tommy Maddox started against the Jaguars. But Tommy Gun jammed, committing four turnovers, including a fumbled snap of a sure-fire winning field goal. In overtime, Jacksonville's Rashean Mathis ran back an interception 41 yards for the winning touchdown.

A wild card team with no home-field advantage, the Steelers had to win three playoff road games to make the Super Bowl. Against division rival Cincinnati in the first game, Ben Roethlisberger threw for three touchdowns as Pittsburgh won 31–17, earning a spot on the cover of Sports Illustrated.

Packers quarterback Brett Favre lies on the ground, watching Troy Polamalu run his fumble back for a 77-yard touchdown. Inspired by Jerome Bettis, Pittsburgh won every game it had to in 2005. When the dust settled, the 11–5 Steelers were headed for the playoffs.

HIGH TIMES AT HEINZ FIELD: 2001–TODAY

On the road in Cincinnati, Ben threw for two touchdowns and Parker rushed for 131 yards en route to a 27–13 victory. On Halloween at Heinz Field, Baltimore's Matt Stover booted three field goals of 40 yards or more in the fourth quarter to give the Ravens a 19–17 lead. But with 1:36 left, Jeff Reed kicked a 37-yard field goal. "It was an ugly win," linebacker Joey Porter said, "but we'll take it."

In Green Bay, the Steelers improved to 6–2 with a 20–10 victory. On one play, safety Troy Polamalu returned a fumble 77 yards for a touchdown. Against the Browns, Antwaan

Win One for The Bus

Jerome Bettis stood to address his teammates. A certain Hall of Famer whose body had taken a terrible beating over the years, Bettis stood with his head bowed. His presence reminded them of all they already knew: how he had taken a pay cut to re-sign with the Steelers because he believed in them, how his role had shrunk to small carries and smaller yardage, how he had carried them for ten years and more than 10,000 yards, busting tackles, getting beaten into the turf. Now, he asked, could they carry him?

After 13 years in the NFL and more than 13,000 rushing yards (more than all but four men in history), there was only one thing he lacked: a championship ring. The 2005 season was his last chance. With Super Bowl XL being played at Ford Field in Detroit, his hometown, he asked: Can you take The Bus home?

"Jerome's our guy," Casey Hampton said. "He asked us to bring him home. That touched us. That's what we fought for."

Then they took him home.

The "Immaculate Redemption" ranks as one of the greatest plays in Steelers history. After picking up Jerome Bettis's late fumble against the Colts in the AFC divisional playoff game, Indy's Nick Harper raced for the end zone. But Big Ben tripped him, leading to the Steelers' 21–18 victory.

Randle El threw a 51-yard TD pass to Hines Ward, highlighting a 34–21 Steelers victory. But then came a three-game tailspin that nearly cost them the season.

In Baltimore, the Ravens sacked Tommy Maddox six times and Stover kicked a 44-yard field goal in overtime, clinching a 16–13 victory. At the RCA Dome, Peyton Manning threw an 80-yard touchdown pass on their first play from scrimmage and Indianapolis never looked back, winning 26–7.

In free fall, the Steelers dropped their third in a row—at home against the Bengals. Cincinnati's defense forced four turnovers, including three Roethlisberger interceptions. After losing 38–31, Cowher said: "We have four games left. We have to play this thing out every week."

In the Heinz Field snow, a reenergized Jerome Bettis plowed through the Bears for his first 100-yard game in a year. Of the 21–9 win, Ward said, "We're desperate. It's a one-game season every week for us. We've got to play like it's the playoffs."

A renowned trash talker, linebacker Joey Porter backed up his taunts with toughness. Here, he corrals Broncos quarterback Jake Plummer in the January 2006 AFC championship game. Four Denver turnovers and three sacks led to a 34–17 Steelers win.

At Minnesota, the Pittsburgh defense recorded a safety, picked off two passes, and blocked a field goal. The Steelers were 9–5, and the AFC wild card looked realistic. "It's do or die now," linebacker James Farrior said. "We have to win. We have to play mistake-free football."

In Cleveland, the Steelers did just that. Parker busted an 80-yard run for a touchdown, the defense sacked rookie quarterback Charlie Frye eight times, and the Steelers won 41–0. On New Year's Day against the Lions, Randle El returned a punt 81 yards for one touchdown and Ricardo Colclough ran back a kick 63 yards to set up another. The Bus scored three short-yardage touchdowns in his final home game. Winning 35–21, Pittsburgh finished 11–5.

If the Steelers were to make it to the Super Bowl, they would have to win three playoff games on the road—a feat no NFL team had ever accomplished. Yet the Steelers looked plenty capable at Cincinnati, as Roethlisberger threw three touchdown passes and no interceptions in a 31–17 victory.

At Indianapolis, the Steelers shocked the 14–2 Colts by taking a 21–3 lead into the fourth quarter. With the score 21–18, Manning was sacked on his own 2-yard line with 1:20 to go. Game over? Far from it. Bettis fumbled on the next play (his first of the season). The Colts' Nick Harper scooped it up and headed for the end zone nearly 100 yards away. Incredibly, Roethlisberger ran him down and grabbed his ankle, with Harper falling on the Indy 42. When the sure-footed Mike Vanderjagt missed a 46-yard field goal, the Steelers escaped with a heart-pounding victory.

"There was no way I could let Jerome's career end that way," Big Ben said.

> "WE TRAVELED A HARD ROAD AND GREW AS A FOOTBALL TEAM. NOW WE NEED TO WIN ONE MORE GAME. NO ONE EVER REMEMBERS WHO LOST THE SUPER BOWL."
>
> BILL COWHER AFTER WINNING THREE PLAYOFF GAMES ON THE ROAD

On the second play of the third quarter in Super Bowl XL, Steelers guard Alan Faneca opened a hole the size of Montana. Running back Willie Parker blew through it for a 75-yard run from scrimmage—the longest in Super Bowl history. The touchdown and extra point gave the Steelers a 14–3 lead over the Seahawks.

HIGH TIMES AT HEINZ FIELD: 2001–TODAY

The Steelers' fourth-quarter gadget play was the hit of every Super Bowl party in Pittsburgh. Ben Roethlisberger handed off to Willie Parker, who handed off to Antwaan Randle El, who fired a strike to Hines Ward, who high-stepped into the end zone for a 43-yard touchdown reception. The Steelers won 21–10.

In Denver, the Steelers played in their sixth AFC championship game in 12 seasons. Roethlisberger, demonstrating uncanny control, completed 21 of 29 for 275 yards and two touchdowns. Pittsburgh scored on its first four possessions, including a touchdown by Bettis, in an easy 34–17 win. The Steelers were on their way to Super Bowl Extra Large to face the Seattle Seahawks.

"We traveled a hard road," Cowher said, "and grew as a football team. Now we need to win one more game. No one ever remembers who lost the Super Bowl."

In Detroit for Super Bowl XL, the jittery, tentative Steelers started slowly. A 47-yard field goal put Seattle up 3–0. After Roethlisberger hit Ward for a 37-yard pass, putting the Steelers on the Seahawks' 3, Bettis picked up two yards and then Ben snuck it in for a touchdown. At the half, the Steelers led 7–3.

On the second play of the third quarter, Pittsburgh guard Alan Faneca opened an enormous hole that allowed Willie Parker to romp 75 yards for a score. It was the longest rushing TD in Super Bowl history, and the Steelers took a 14–3 lead.

With the score 14–10, Ike Taylor intercepted a Matt Hasselbeck pass. A few plays later, with the ball at the Seahawks' 43, the Steelers rocked the house with the greatest gadget play in team history. Roethlisberger pitched to Parker, who handed off to wide receiver Randel El—the former All-America quarterback for Indiana. Randle El fired a perfect strike to a wide-open Ward at the 5, and he ran it in to make it 20–10. The extra point ended the scoring.

After 14 seasons with the Steelers and ten trips to the playoffs, coach Bill Cowher had finally achieved the ultimate dream—his first Super Bowl victory, and the fifth in team history.

Afterward, a beaming Cowher handed the Lombardi Trophy to Dan Rooney. Was it the long-anticipated "one for the thumb"?

"This is a new group," Rooney said, "a new time. This isn't one for the thumb. It's one for these guys."

Victory at last! Every coach's dream was Bill Cowher's reality on February 5, 2006, when Cowher won his first Super Bowl and hoisted the Vince Lombardi Trophy. Moments later, Cowher turned to his chairman and said, "Mr. Rooney, this is for you."

PITTSBURGH STEELERS YESTERDAY & TODAY

Cowher's Farewell Season

In 2006, the air went out of the balloon.

Hoping to begin another dynasty, hoping to be the first Steelers team to repeat as Super Bowl champs since 1978–79, the Black and Gold went a desultory 8–8, finishing out of the playoffs and then losing their coach.

The star-crossed season was marred by Ben Roethlisberger's June 2006 motorcycle accident, then his appendectomy, and finally his concussions. On top of that, every team in the league was gunning for the reigning Super Bowl champs.

Looking back on a mediocre season, nose tackle Chris Hoke told the *Pittsburgh Post-Gazette,* "I don't think it's because we weren't hungry. We practiced hard, we prepared for each game as we did in the past. We had the whole thing with Ben. We had other injuries."

After winning the opener with Charlie Batch at quarterback, the Steelers lost six of their next seven games, all with Big Ben in the starting lineup. Although the Steelers went 6–2 in the second half, it was too little, too late.

Then, 11 months after winning Super Bowl XL, Bill Cowher retired.

Perhaps the best way to describe his 15-year tenure as Steelers coach is to note what went on around him. From 1992 to 2006, 105 NFL head coaches were hired. In the same period, the Steelers posted the NFL's best regular-season record, 149–90–1. Making the playoffs ten seasons, Cowher won eight division titles, played in six AFC championship games, and won one Super Bowl in two tries.

"History will look back on Bill Cowher as one of the great head coaches of his time," Dan Rooney said. "He led us through one of the most successful eras in franchise history and has my lasting respect and admiration."

It wasn't all bad news in 2006. Although the Steelers went 8–8, Willie Parker scored 16 touchdowns, rushed for 100 yards seven times, and amassed 1,494 yards rushing on the season—including 223 of them in this game against the Browns on December 7.

Big Ben's Brush with Death

Bill Cowher warned him about it, and so did Terry Bradshaw. But Ben, being Ben, didn't listen.

On June 12, 2006, Roethlisberger—notorious for riding his 2005 Suzuki Hayabusa without a helmet—was hit by a Chrysler New Yorker near the Steelers' practice facility. After flying into the car's windshield and crashing on the pavement, Roethlisberger underwent life-saving treatment by paramedics before being taken to Mercy Hospital. He endured seven hours of surgery for multiple facial fractures, a nine-inch head gash, lost and chipped teeth, and the ruptured blood vessel that nearly killed him.

Remains of Roethlisberger's motorcycle

Three days later, an apologetic Roethlisberger said, "If I ever ride again, it certainly will be with a helmet."

Banged up, Ben nevertheless started the first three preseason games.

Whew.

Tales of the Terrible Towel

Hung from Mount Everest and the Great Wall of China, taken to the South Pole and Vatican City, rocketed by Pittsburgher Mike Fincke to the International Space Station, flown by Air Force jets over Afghanistan, spun at Super Bowls and on *Saturday Night Live,* the Terrible Towel is the nation's most recognizable sports banner.

The creation of late broadcaster Myron Cope, the Terrible Towel was born in 1975. Asked to come up with a gimmick for the fans, Cope protested that he wasn't a gimmick guy—and neither was the team. Pressured to do *something,* Cope figured that a small towel was perfect. It was something everyone could buy or scrounge from the kitchen. It was easily manipulated, instantly democratic. It immediately conferred membership on anyone who hoisted one.

For weeks, Cope screeched on the air, "The Terrible Towel is poised to strike!" All the while, many Steelers players were predicting that the promotion would fall flat.

Born of a 1975 gimmick, Myron Cope's Terrible Towel became the Steelers' symbol. Here, the faithful twirl their Terrible Towels before the Monday night game against the hated Ravens on October 31, 2005, when the Steelers honored Cope himself.

The Terrible Towels made their debut on December 27, 1975, when 30,000 fans waved them proudly during a playoff victory over the Colts. The next week, Lynn Swann came out of the runway waving one.

The tradition was picked up by succeeding generations of Steelers fans. An estimated six million Terrible Towels have been sold, raising $3 million for the Allegheny Valley School in nearby Coraopolis. The facility cares for the mentally disabled, including Cope's own son, Danny.

"I think every great nation has a flag," Pittsburgh safety Troy Polamalu said, as quoted on ESPN.com. "I think [for] the Steeler Nation, it's obvious that's our flag."

Not everyone, however, has treated the Terrible Towel with such reverence—although the disrespectful have paid the price. For example, before a 1994 playoff game against the Browns, Cleveland running back Earnest Byner stepped on the Towel. The Steelers won 29–9.

During a December 4, 2005, game at Heinz Field, Bengal T. J. Houshmandzadeh scored—then wiped his feet on the Towel. Although they won that game, the Bengals lost to the Black and Gold in the playoffs.

Before the September 29, 2008, game at Heinz Field, Raven Derrick Mason stomped on the Towel. The Ravens lost all three 2008 season games to the Steelers, including the AFC championship game.

The ultimate revenge came later that season after Phoenix's mayor had the Cardinals mascot wipe his armpits with the Towel before the mayor blew his nose on it. The Cardinals lost Super Bowl XLIII to the Steelers.

An insult too great to bear! Tennessee Titans defensive end Jevon Kearse blows his nose on a Terrible Towel before the December 21, 2008, game in Nashville. To make matters worse, the Titans won 31–14—although they lost in the first round of the playoffs to Baltimore.

"When they wave that towel," Ben Roethlisberger said, as quoted on ESPN.com, "it's just something that comes from their soul and tries to reach out to us players."

Tomlin Takes the Reins

He was young, Mike Tomlin, just 34, and he beat long odds to win one of football's most coveted positions—head coach of the Pittsburgh Steelers.

In an organization famous for stability—one family had owned the team since 1933, just two head coaches since 1969—Tomlin took the prize in January 2007. He was named head coach a little more than a year after the team won its fifth Super Bowl and a month after the team concluded an 8–8 season.

"The main thing you think about," Art Rooney II told the *Pittsburgh Post-Gazette,* "is when this guy is standing up in front of your team, is he going to be able to get his message across? I think that is what convinced us that this is the guy."

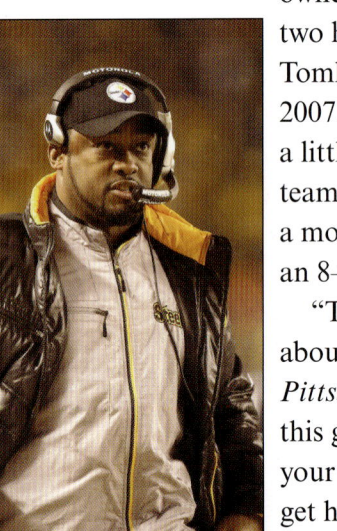

Cool, canny, and communicative, Steelers head coach Mike Tomlin catapulted from college coaching to the NFL. Trained in part by Tampa Bay head coach Tony Dungy, who happened to be trained by Pittsburgh's Chuck Noll, Tomlin needed just two seasons to lead the Steelers to the Super Bowl.

While many fans and players rooted for coach Wiz—popular offensive coordinator Ken Whisenhunt—to replace retired Bill Cowher, the Steelers interviewed Tomlin, then the Vikings' defensive coordinator. Famous for demoting stars if they dogged it, Tomlin had motivated his men to unprecedented achievement.

Lack of motivation is what he faced entering the 2007 season. With the Steelers out of the money a year earlier and bereft of team leadership, who knew how bad the team's tailspin would be? At worst, the Steelers would face another decade like the 1980s. Fortunately, the new coach was up to the task. Tomlin, a former receiver at William & Mary, had enjoyed a meteoric rise in coaching. At 28, he made Tony Dungy's staff in Tampa Bay. He seemed fit for the challenge in Pittsburgh.

"We intend to make no bold predictions about what we're going to do," Tomlin told the *Post-Gazette.* "What we are going to do is promise to have a first-class, blue-collar work ethic in how we approach our business."

"We've got some quality players," he added. "I'm sure the recent Super Bowl success—and the failure that followed—will make them a hungry group of men."

Ownership Shake-up

When the smoke cleared, Dan Rooney and Art II still led the Steelers. After Super Bowl XL, NFL Commissioner Roger Goodell announced that the Steelers must comply with NFL rules on majority control and gambling. The Chief, who had divided his Steelers holdings between his five sons, also had given them racetracks. Now, Dan and Art II (as majority owners) had to own 30 percent of the team stock, and no owner could have gambling interests.

Art Rooney II (left) and Dan Rooney

Some Rooneys sold some of their Steelers stock, others sold all of it, and outside investors were secured in 2008 and ratified in '09.

Named team president in 2002, Art Rooney II said that succeeding two Hall of Famers "is a privilege and an honor. But it's not as if I'm following people that I didn't know."

HIGH TIMES AT HEINZ FIELD: 2001–TODAY

Ten Wins and a Quick Playoff Exit

"We don't live in our fears," Mike Tomlin said after beating the St. Louis Rams on December 20, 2007, "we live in our hopes."

Nothing better describes Tomlin's rookie year with the Steelers. In Pittsburgh's 75th season, he had to play behind Bill Cowher's victorious Super Bowl XL—and overcome the desultory 8–8 season of 2006.

Undaunted, Tomlin took a team full of talent—Ben Roethlisberger, Hines Ward, Willie Parker; James Harrison, James Farrior, Troy Polamalu—and led them back to the playoffs.

After trouncing Cleveland 34–7 on the road, and then walloping the Bills 26–3 and the 49ers 37–16 at home, the 3–0 Steelers looked invincible. But in Arizona, the Cardinals outlasted Pittsburgh 21–14. Back home, the Steelers shut out the Seahawks, their Super Bowl XL rivals, 21–0.

Pittsburgh lost at Denver 31–28, but a 24–13 win against the Bengals in Cincinnati sent Steelers spirits soaring. So did Pittsburgh's 38–7 dismantling of the Ravens and 31–28 victory over the Browns.

Facing the Jets in Jersey, the 7–2 Steelers were unable to hold the lead. A Jets field goal took it to OT, where New York won 19–16. At Heinz Field on Monday night, Pittsburgh and the 0–10 Dolphins couldn't get it going in the pouring rain—until, with 17 seconds left, Jeff Reed kicked a 24-yard field goal for a 3–0 Steelers win.

Starved for points, the Steelers ate the Bengals 24–10, with Ward surpassing John Stallworth for most touchdown receptions by a Steeler. Although 9–3, the Steelers were overmatched at New England. Trailing 17–13 at the half, Pittsburgh was shut out the rest of the way, losing 34–13 to a team that would go 16–0. Trailing the Jaguars by 15 going into the fourth quarter, the Steelers fought valiantly, but a Jacksonville TD clinched a 29–22 Jaguars victory.

While mauling the Rams in St. Louis 41–24, Ward passed Stallworth for most receiving yards by a Steeler. Meanwhile, Parker broke his leg, ending a 1,316-yard season. Though the Ravens picked the Steelers' bones in Baltimore 27–21 to close the season, Pittsburgh finished at 10–6 to win the AFC North.

At Heinz Field, the Steelers faced the Jaguars in the AFC wild card game—and lost. Trailing 28–10 in the fourth quarter, Roethlisberger orchestrated three touchdown drives to put Pittsburgh up 29–28. But a Josh Scobee chip-shot field goal with 37 seconds left won it for the Jags 31–29.

Jeff Reed misses a field goal during the rain-soaked game against the hapless Dolphins on Monday, November 26, 2007. Later in the game, with just seconds left, Reed kicked a 24-yard field goal for a 3–0 Steelers victory. Pittsburgh went 10–6 and made the playoffs.

In an AFC wild card game in January 2008, Pittsburgh's Carey Davis reacts to dropping what should have been a touchdown pass in the fourth quarter. Jacksonville won the game with a field goal 31–29.

STEELERS MEMORIES

Although this button calls it the "Immaculate Tackle," it is better known as the "Immaculate Redemption." Ben Roethlisberger prevented the Colts' Nick Harper from scoring the winning touchdown in the 2006 playoffs.

Heath's Big Money Bar—named for Steelers tight end Heath Miller—is right on target. Miller has earned a reputation as a "money" player for getting important first downs and touchdowns.

Carla Leman holds a Big Ben Burger in Tony's Restaurant in Findlay, Ohio, Roethlisberger's hometown. Many of the town's Bengals and Browns fans changed their allegiance to the Steelers when Big Ben became an NFL star.

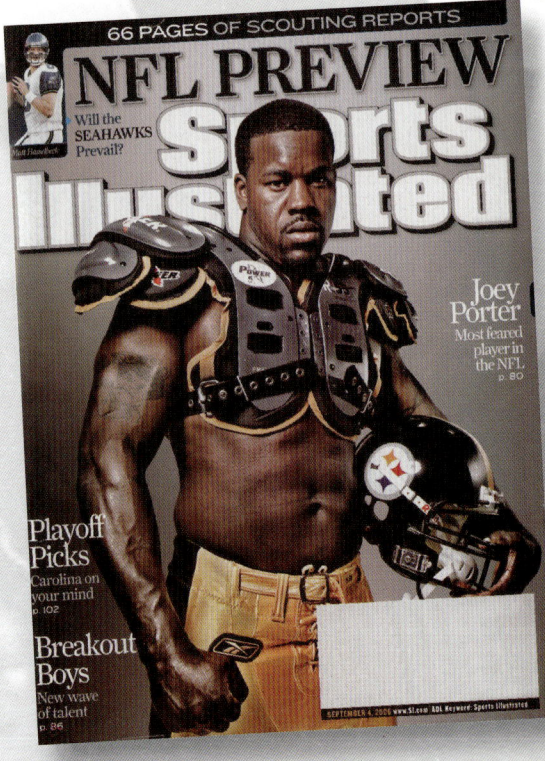

Joey Porter flexes his muscles on the cover of Sports Illustrated. On a team of incredibly sculpted athletes, the 6'3", 255-pound Porter may have had the manliest physique.

The Steelers commemorated their 75th anniversary by having fans vote on an all-time team. Among the chosen were Bradshaw, Bettis, and Bleier; Stallworth, Swann, and Ward; Lambert, Ham, and Russell; and Greene, Greenwood, and Woodson.

President George W. Bush hosts the Steelers at the White House on June 2, 2006. The President said that Dick Cheney had asked him to get some tips regarding the scowl that Bill Cowher often wore on the sidelines.

An idle thought by singer Roger Wood became the club's unofficial anthem. Pictured here at a Heinz Field pre-Super Bowl pep rally, Wood sang "Here We Go! The Steeler Fight Song."

All of Steeler Nation celebrated Pittsburgh's victory in Super Bowl XL. Hines Ward, the game's MVP, was featured on the front page of the *Pittsburgh Tribune-Review*.

PITTSBURGH STEELERS YESTERDAY & TODAY

Sixburgh!

In 2007, rookie head coach Mike Tomlin proved his mettle by winning the AFC North title. What would he do for an encore?

With the NFL's most difficult schedule, reaching higher would be difficult. But, Tomlin answered, "iron sharpens iron."

Opening at Heinz Field against the Texans, the Steelers scored on their first three possessions and never looked back. Willie Parker scored three times, and LaMarr Woodley's interception set up a Hines Ward touchdown. En route to winning the NFL Defensive Player of the Year Award, linebacker James Harrison recorded three sacks. The final: 38–17 Pittsburgh.

On a windy day in Cleveland, a Ben Roethlisberger to Hines Ward touchdown pass was the only TD of the day, as Pittsburgh won 10–6. The next week, the 2–0 Steelers stalled in Philadelphia. Although the Black and Gold again scored on their first drive, they were unable to rein in Donovan McNabb—or stop the Eagles from sacking Big Ben. With Roethlisberger on the deck eight times, the Steelers lost 15–6.

Facing the Ravens on Monday night at Heinz Field, Pittsburgh traded field goals with Baltimore before two first-round draft picks exploded for scores. Roethlisberger fired a 38-yarder to Santonio Holmes, and Woodley scored when he picked up Harrison's forced fumble and ran it in. Although the Ravens tied it at 20, Pittsburgh's Jeff Reed kicked a 46-yard field goal in overtime for a 23–20 victory.

At Jacksonville, the 3–1 Steelers and the Jaguars traded leads until the Steelers prevailed 26–21. In Cincinnati, the Steelers once again scored on their first possession and then put the game away with an explosive three-TD fourth quarter. They won 38–10.

Hosting the world champion Giants, Pittsburgh scored on the opening drive on a Mewelde Moore 32-yard touchdown run. Down 14–12 in the fourth quarter, New York tied the game on a bad-snap safety and wound up winning 21–14. The Steelers, however, rebounded the next week with an easy 23–6

Featured on the cover of ESPN The Magazine, *the awesome 2008 Steelers defense accounted for 51 sacks, 20 interceptions, 12 forced fumbles, and 22 fumble recoveries. Their 223 points allowed was the lowest total in the NFL.*

Linebacker James Harrison, the 2008 NFL Defensive Player of the Year, puts one of his patented hurts on Patriots quarterback Matt Cassel, who coughs up the ball. Behind the crushing Steelers defense, Pittsburgh defeated New England 33–10 in this November 30, 2008, game and finished at 12–4.

win over the Redskins to improve to 6–2. In a marquee match-up with Indianapolis at home, Pittsburgh broke a 17–17 tie with a field goal in the fourth quarter. But Peyton Manning proved the difference, as his third touchdown pass moved the Colts ahead; they won 24–20.

With the Steelers trailing the Chargers 7–0 at Heinz, Harrison forced a fumble in the end zone for a safety, making it 7–2. Two Reed field goals gave the Steelers an odd 8–7 lead, and a Chargers field goal gave them the advantage at 10–8. But another Reed boot made it 11–10 Steelers, where it stayed. Not only did Pittsburgh win without scoring a touchdown, but it was the first 11–10 game in NFL history.

The next game, the Steelers did what they do best—beat the Bengals, 27–10. After falling behind early at New England, Pittsburgh put up 30 unanswered points. With the resounding 33–10 victory, the team improved to 9–3.

With the Cowboys in town, the Steelers nearly let one slip away. But with Dallas up 13–3 in the fourth quarter, Reed booted a field goal and Big Ben connected with Heath Miller to tie the game with 2:04 left. The Steelers won 20–14 after Deshea Townsend returned an interception for a touchdown.

In Baltimore, with the Ravens leading 9–6 in the fourth quarter, a four-yard touchdown pass by Roethlisberger to Holmes capped a 92-yard drive and clinched a 13–9 victory. For the 11–3 Steelers, it also clinched their second consecutive AFC North title. However, a 31–14 butt whipping by the 12–2 Titans showed that Pittsburgh was by no means the alpha team in the AFC.

The Steelers closed the regular season at Heinz Field against the Browns, who should have stayed in Cleveland. The Steelers crushed them 31–0 to finish at 12–4. For the season, the Pittsburgh defense yielded just 13.9 points per game, tops in the NFL.

With Pittsburgh hosting the Chargers in the AFC divisional game, Santonio Holmes rocked the house with a 67-yard punt return for a touchdown. A Parker touchdown made it 14–10, and Heath Miller, Gary Russell, and Parker touchdowns iced the game 35–24.

The High-Rent District

With six Super Bowl victories, the Steelers rank with the Yankees, Celtics, and Canadiens among the sports world's elite teams.

Super Bowl Victories
Pittsburgh Steelers	6
Dallas Cowboys	5
San Francisco 49ers	5

World Series Titles
New York Yankees	27
St. Louis Cardinals	10
Philadelphia/Oakland A's	9

NBA Championships
Boston Celtics	17
Los Angeles Lakers	15
Chicago Bulls	6

Stanley Cup Titles
Montreal Canadiens	24
Toronto Maple Leafs	13
Detroit Red Wings	11

Fancy meeting you here! Nate Washington and Santonio Holmes celebrate Holmes's punt return for a touchdown against San Diego in a divisional playoff game in January 2009. This 67-yard run tied the game, and the Steelers cruised 35–24.

PITTSBURGH STEELERS YESTERDAY & TODAY

Some said the crowd's roar was the loudest thing they had ever heard. Against the Ravens in the AFC championship game, with the score 16–14 Steelers, Troy Polamalu picked off a pass and ran it back for a 40-yard touchdown, icing the game 23–14.

With No. 1 seed Tennessee eliminated, the Steelers hosted the Ravens in the AFC championship game. A pair of Jeff Reed field goals and a Holmes touchdown catch gave Pittsburgh a 13–0 lead. With the home team up 16–14, Troy Polamalu intercepted a pass and took it 40 yards for a Steelers score, securing a 23–14 win. For the second time in four years, the Steelers were AFC champions.

In the depths of a recession, Steelers fans nonetheless flocked to Super Bowl XLIII in Tampa, Florida. The Steelers were heavy favorites against the Super Bowl–virgin Cardinals, who had snuck into the playoffs at 9–7. After an 18-yard Reed field goal, a one-yard Russell TD run, and an Arizona score, Pittsburgh led 10–7. Then, on the final play of the first half, James Harrison pulled off the "Immaculate Interception," returning a pass 100 yards for a touchdown—the longest play in Super Bowl history.

A chip-shot field goal by Reed was the only score in the third quarter, after which Pittsburgh led 20–7. But the Super Bowl partiers who went home early missed an extraordinary fourth quarter. After an 87-yard Cardinals touchdown drive cut the lead to 20–14, Steelers center Justin Hartwig was penalized for holding in his end zone, costing Pittsburgh a safety. Then, with less than three minutes remaining, Larry

On the final play of the first half of Super Bowl XLIII, James Harrison picked off a Cardinals pass on the goal line and ran it back 100 yards for a touchdown—fending off defenders all the way down the field. The Steelers led at the half 17–7.

HIGH TIMES AT HEINZ FIELD: 2001–TODAY

In a play that Steelers fans will remember forever, Santonio Holmes keeps his toes in the end zone as he catches a touchdown pass with 35 seconds left in Super Bowl XLIII. The Steelers went up 27–23 to win their record sixth Super Bowl.

Holmes was named the game's MVP, but coach Mike Tomlin knew it was a complete team effort. "I'm proud of the sacrifices and the accomplishments of the men involved," Tomlin said, "but it was something I thought we were capable of. I wouldn't want to have won this any other way, with everybody contributing to that trophy case."

Fitzgerald caught a Kurt Warner pass on a post pattern for a stunning 64-yard scoring play. Arizona now led 23–20.

After a holding penalty, the Steelers found themselves 88 yards from the end zone with just over two minutes left. But Big Ben had a big weapon: Santonio Holmes. Four times on the drive he connected with his dazzling wideout, including a thrilling 40-yard pass play that put the ball on the Cardinals' 6-yard line. Two plays later, with less than 40 seconds remaining, Holmes hauled in a pass in the corner of the end zone, with both feet barely in bounds, for one of the greatest clutch catches in football history. The Steelers led 27–23.

Arizona reached the Steelers' 44 in a matter of seconds. But a fumble-inducing sack by Woodley and Brett Keisel's fumble recovery ended one of the most exciting Super Bowls of all time.

Darnell Stapleton holds *The Tampa Tribune* as he joins his teammates—and millions of Steelers fans—in celebrating the team's second Super Bowl victory in four years. Two days later, fans jammed the parade route to share the team's joy.

PITTSBURGH STEELERS YESTERDAY & TODAY

Stars of the New Millennium

The Steelers are known around the NFL as a model organization—supreme management and coaching, strong team unity, and a commitment to excellence. All of these factors have contributed to their two Super Bowls in the new millennium, but let's not forget: The Steelers also have been loaded with talent.

In addition to quarterback Ben Roethlisberger and receiver Hines Ward—elite players at their positions—Pro Bowl players have lined up all over the field for the Steelers.

Five-time Pro Bowl strong safety **Troy Polamalu** has redefined his position. Strong, quick, and seemingly able to fly, Polamalu adds range and power to the Steelers' defense. A 2003 first-round pick, he excels at hard hits, tackles, and interceptions, including seven in 2008.

The classic scatback (rare on a team that has favored power backs), 5'10", 209-pound running back **Willie Parker** has superb moves and 4.3 speed. Capable of eluding defenders at will, Parker perfectly complements the Steelers' aerial circus. "Fast Willie," who was signed as an undrafted free agent, became a Steelers starter in 2005. He was named team MVP in 2006, when he scored 16 touchdowns and rushed for 1,494 yards, third most in Steelers history.

No one ever doubted linebacker **Joey Porter's** intensity—or willingness to express himself. From 1999 to 2006, he was the Steelers' big-play, big-hit motivator, with his tackles accompanied by his trademark post-play "place-kick." A four-time Pro Bowler, Porter piled up 60 sacks in eight years.

Another powerful player, two-time Pro Bowl linebacker **James Farrior** (as in warrior) arrived as a free agent in 2002. The Steelers MVP in 2004, Farrior led the team for the third consecutive season in tackles in 2008 (146, including 100 solo) and surpassed 1,200 for his career.

The 2008 NFL Defensive Player of the Year, linebacker **James Harrison** capped his outstanding season with the "Immaculate Interception" (the 100-yard dash to the end zone) in the Super Bowl. The 6'0", 240-pounder joined the team as a rookie free agent in 2002. Released twice, he made the Steelers' roster and worked his way up from special teams. The epitome of grit and determination, Harrison set the single-season Steelers sacks record with 16 in 2008.

With enough muscle for an entire squad, linebacker Joey Porter always seemed to find a way to get to the quarterback—and inflict maximum damage. Adding post-play panache, he celebrates another big hit in the January 2005 AFC championship game.

Safety Troy Polamalu, featured on the cover of Sports Illustrated, *has been a nightmare for barbers and quarterbacks. Blessed with superhuman speed (4.35 in the 40) and hops (43-inch vertical leap), Polamalu amasses both sacks and interceptions.*

Some 325 pounds—on an Ultra Slim Fast day—nose tackle **Casey Hampton** nevertheless is as quick as a cat. A major asset in the Steelers' defensive line, the '01 first-round pick has earned two championship rings and four Pro Bowl invitations. Hampton's leadership skills are quiet and understated, yet greatly respected around the NFL.

Smart, strong, and a seven-time Pro Bowl selection as a Steeler, guard **Alan Faneca** was a first-round pick in 1998 who anchored the offensive line for a decade. Although statistics for guards are impossible to generate, the Steelers' rushers and passers saw unprecedented opportunity on Faneca's watch.

The definition of the big-impact rookie, linebacker **Kendrell Bell** arrived in the second round in 2001 and outplayed most of those drafted ahead of him. The NFL Defensive Rookie of the Year, Bell set a Steelers freshman record with nine sacks. Up through 2004, when he was injured, Bell started 44 games, recorded 239 tackles, and logged 18 sacks.

At 6'5" and 300 pounds, defensive end **Aaron Smith** is the textbook impact player. The 1999 fourth-round pick blossomed into a durable lineman and a sack specialist. Named to the Pro Bowl in 2004 after a career-high eight sacks, he entered 2009 with 42 QB crunchers.

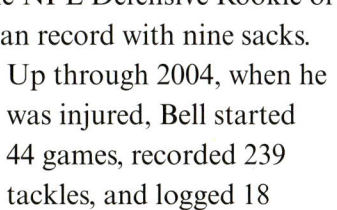

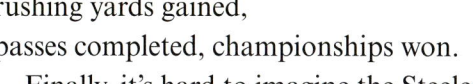

Weighing in at roughly one-sixth of a ton, defensive nose tackle Casey Hampton looks like a mountain—but moves like an avalanche. That's Oakland's Adam Treu trying in vain to get a handle on No. 98.

Goodbye and good luck: Guard Alan Faneca says farewell to Steelers fans after an AFC wild card game on January 5, 2008. After anchoring the offensive line for ten years, the articulate, affable Faneca was a fan and player favorite.

Center **Jeff Hartings**, another strong Steelers lineman, arrived as a free agent in 2001. In six years in Pittsburgh, Hartings played in two Pro Bowls. As with Alan Faneca, Hartings's statistics belong to his teammates— rushing yards gained, passes completed, championships won.

Finally, it's hard to imagine the Steelers' Super Bowl XLIII victory without wide receiver and kick returner **Santonio Holmes**, who took MVP honors thanks to his game-winning touchdown catch. A first-round pick in 2006, Holmes possesses exceptional speed and great hands. In his first three years, he amassed 2,587 yards receiving and 15 touchdown catches.

Who will continue to shine? "Change is part of this business," coach Mike Tomlin said. "Sometimes it's going to be more unpleasant than others, but it's the nature of what we do. This group understands the standard that comes with being a Pittsburgh Steeler."

Falling Short in '09

How ignoble it was when the reigning Super Bowl champions had to watch the scoreboard, hoping for a near-impossible set of losses so they could sneak into the playoffs.

As the new century's first decade drew to a close, the Steelers limped to a 9–7 record. To crudely paraphrase Charles Dickens: It was a season for the record books, it was a season for the Dumpster.

First, the records. For the first time in the same season, the team had two 1,000-yard receivers (Santonio Holmes and Hines Ward, who also became the team's first 10,000-yard receiver), a 1,000-yard rusher (sophomore Rashard Mendenhall), and a 4,000-yard passer (team MVP Ben Roethlisberger). To burnish his image, Big Ben also set the Steelers' single-game passing record, throwing for a whopping 503 yards (tenth most in NFL history) against Green Bay.

The potent offense helped the Steelers win six of their first eight games. So how did a 6–2 team go into a five-loss tailspin, with the inferior Raiders, Chiefs, and Browns slapping the Steelers silly? Age hurt, as did injuries, especially the loss of safety Troy Polamalu. As the popular T-shirt says: Two-thirds of the Earth is covered by water. The rest is covered by Troy Polamalu.

At times, the squad seemed to lose focus. More than once, the kickoff coverage seemed to be in another stadium, and the offensive line was inconsistent. In Cleveland, the Browns dumped Ben eight gut-wrenching times.

After a galling loss in Cincinnati, when the Steelers blew a 20–9 fourth-quarter lead to lose 23–20, offensive tackle Willie Colon described what would become the problem for the rest of 2009: "We have to finish games. We're not doing the little things, and it's catching up to us. If we don't change, it's going to be a rotten season."

There were bright spots. First-round draft choice Ziggy Hood earned his spurs, while James Harrison and Casey Hampton both returned to the Pro Bowl. Linebacker LaMarr Woodley stepped up big-time. Against the Ravens, for example, he recorded ten tackles, two sacks, and a forced fumble. "He's been that kind of guy

Ben Roethlisberger was sacked eight times in this game against the 1–11 Browns. The shocking 13–6 defeat was the Steelers' fifth loss in a row—tied for the most ever by a reigning Super Bowl champion.

since he's been here," coach Mike Tomlin said about his sophomore star. "He's a guy that's on the rise."

Opening the season, the Steelers gained just 36 yards on the ground but outlasted Tennessee in overtime 13–10. Against the Bears in Chicago, the Steelers came up a field goal shy, losing 17–14. Then the Steelers dropped another one, again by three points, to the Bengals in Cincinnati, 23–20. "The Super Bowl champions starting 1–2," Hines Ward said. "It's not what we envisioned."

With Green Bay up 36–30, Ben Roethlisberger hits receiver Mike Wallace as time expires. The extra point made it 37–36 Pittsburgh and kept the Steelers (7–7) in the playoff hunt.

They followed up, however, with five wins in a row. Pittsburgh beat the Chargers 38–28, although the 21 points that the Steelers yielded in the fourth quarter were troubling. The following week, Pittsburgh had to fight another fourth-quarter surge to hold off the woeful Lions 28–20. At Heinz Field, the Steelers crushed the Browns 27–14.

Now on a roll, Pittsburgh took out the 6–0 Vikings 27–17, then whipped 6–1 Denver 28–10. The 6–2 Steelers looked unstoppable.

Then came the free fall, with the team dropping five in a row for the first time since 2003. First, the playoff-bound Bengals mauled the Steelers 18–12 at Heinz Field, and then the Black and Gold lost 27–24 in overtime to the 2–7 Chiefs. "I take responsibility for that performance," Tomlin said. "I have to have this football team better prepared to play."

He didn't. Another overtime game, against the Ravens, resulted in another loss, 20–17, after the Steelers were again unable to hold a fourth-quarter lead. In a can't-lose game against 3–8 Oakland, Pittsburgh let another close one slip away, 27–24, giving up 21 points in the now-fatal fourth quarter. The Steelers were the talk of the NFL when they dropped their fifth in a row, 13–6 to the 1–11 Cleveland Browns. The reigning champions were now 6–7.

With only faint hopes for the playoffs still alive, Pittsburgh outlasted Green Bay, as Roethlisberger's touchdown pass to rookie Mike Wallace as time expired led to a nail-biting 37–36 win. "We've got a little pulse here," Tomlin said.

After improving to 8–7 with a 23–20 win over the Ravens, Pittsburgh defeated the Dolphins 30–24 to close out the season at 9–7. Two AFC teams made the playoffs with that record, but the Steelers lost out on tiebreakers. Still, their coach was impressed with the strong finish. "I have a great deal of respect for our football team," Tomlin said, "not only in terms of their closeness, but their willingness to fight."

The Steelers would need to retain that fighting spirit for a *full* season if they were to return to contention in 2010.

STEELERS MEMORIES

With the 2008 AFC championship game looming, Pittsburgh Mayor Luke Ravenstahl had his office door changed. He crossed out Ravens and replaced it with Steelers, thereby becoming Mayor Steelerstahl.

As the *Pittsburgh Tribune-Review* trumpeted on its front page, the Steelers were in sole possession of six Super Bowl trophies. Here, Super Bowl MVP Santonio Holmes hoists the most recent piece of history.

The Steeler fan's ultimate dream: a six-pack of Lombardi trophies. The thinking behind this photo coincides with the old bumper sticker that said, "Pittsburgh: a drinking town with a football problem."

Santonio Holmes went to Disney World to celebrate the Super Bowl XLIII victory. He even got to ride with Mickey Mouse in a parade, which featured football-shaped black-and-gold balloons.

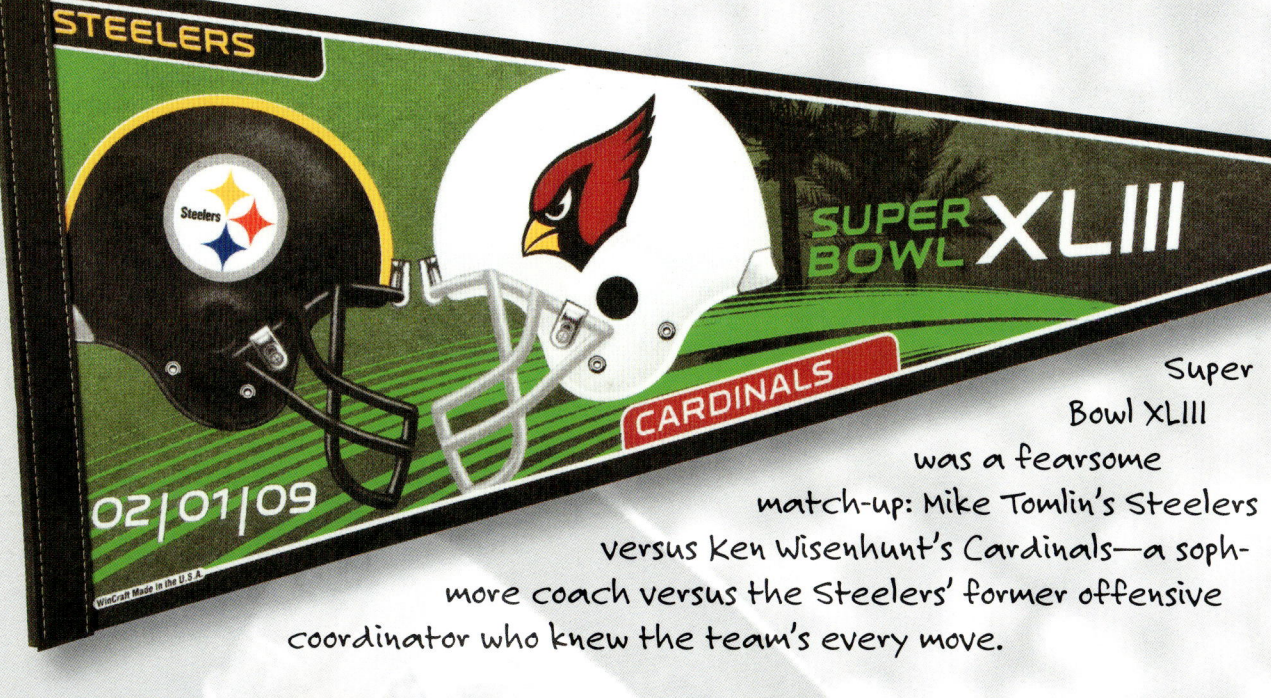

Super Bowl XLIII was a fearsome match-up: Mike Tomlin's Steelers versus Ken Wisenhunt's Cardinals—a sophmore coach versus the Steelers' former offensive coordinator who knew the team's every move.

After waiting 26 years for the fifth ring ("One for the Thumb" took from 1980 to 2006), the Steelers needed just three more years to get a ring for the other hand.

These big-headed dolls (with movable joints) celebrate a quartet of Super Bowl XLIII champions: Ben Roethlisberger, Hines Ward, Troy Polamalu, and James Harrison.

The Steelers' Super Bowl XLIII victory parade in downtown Pittsburgh drew an estimated 400,000 people. Here, James Harrison—who made the "Immaculate Interception"—holds aloft Pittsburgh's sixth Lombardi Trophy.

CHAPTER FIVE

STEELERS BY THE NUMBERS

Pittsburgh Steelers in the NFL

Year	Coach	Record	Place/Title	Year	Coach	Record	Place/Title
1933	Forrest Douds	3–6–2	5th	1959	Buddy Parker	6–5–1	4th
1934	Luby DiMelio	2–10	5th	1960	Buddy Parker	5–6–1	5th
1935	Joe Bach	4–8	3rd	1961	Buddy Parker	6–8	5th
1936	Joe Bach	6–6	2nd	1962	Buddy Parker	9–5	2nd
1937	John McNally	4–7	3rd	1963	Buddy Parker	7–4–3	4th
1938	John McNally	2–9	5th	1964	Buddy Parker	5–9	6th
1939	John McNally/Walt Kiesling	1–9–1	4th	1965	Mike Nixon	2–12	7th
1940	Walt Kiesling	2–7–2	4th	1966	Bill Austin	5–8–1	6th
1941	Bert Bell/Aldo Donelli/Walt Kiesling	1–9–1	5th	1967	Bill Austin	4–9–1	4th
1942	Walt Kiesling	7–4	2nd	1968	Bill Austin	2–11–1	4th
1943	Walt Kiesling/Earle Neale	5–4–1	3rd	1969	Chuck Noll	1–13	4th
1944	Walt Kiesling/Phil Handler	0–10	5th	1970	Chuck Noll	5–9	3rd
1945	Jim Leonard	2–8	5th	1971	Chuck Noll	6–8	2nd
1946	Jock Sutherland	5–5–1	3rd	1972	Chuck Noll	11–3	1st/AFC Central champions
1947	Jock Sutherland	8–4	1st	1973	Chuck Noll	10–4	1st/AFC Central co-champions
1948	John Michelosen	4–8	3rd	1974	Chuck Noll	10–3–1	1st/Super Bowl champions
1949	John Michelosen	6–5–1	2nd	1975	Chuck Noll	12–2	1st/Super Bowl champions
1950	John Michelosen	6–6	3rd	1976	Chuck Noll	10–4	1st/AFC Central co-champions
1951	John Michelosen	4–7–1	4th	1977	Chuck Noll	9–5	1st/AFC Central champions
1952	Joe Bach	5–7	4th	1978	Chuck Noll	14–2	1st/Super Bowl champions
1953	Joe Bach	6–6	4th	1979	Chuck Noll	12–4	1st/Super Bowl champions
1954	Walt Kiesling	5–7	4th	1980	Chuck Noll	9–7	3rd
1955	Walt Kiesling	4–8	6th	1981	Chuck Noll	8–8	2nd
1956	Walt Kiesling	5–7	4th	1982	Chuck Noll	6–3	4th
1957	Buddy Parker	6–6	3rd	1983	Chuck Noll	10–6	1st/AFC Central champions
1958	Buddy Parker	7–4–1	3rd	1984	Chuck Noll	9–7	1st/AFC Central champions
				1985	Chuck Noll	7–9	2nd

STEELERS BY THE NUMBERS

Year	Coach	Record	Place/Title
1986	Chuck Noll	6–10	3rd
1987	Chuck Noll	8–7	3rd
1988	Chuck Noll	5–11	4th
1989	Chuck Noll	9–7	2nd
1990	Chuck Noll	9–7	1st/AFC Central co-champions
1991	Chuck Noll	7–9	2nd
1992	Bill Cowher	11–5	1st/AFC Central champions
1993	Bill Cowher	9–7	2nd
1994	Bill Cowher	12–4	1st/AFC Central champions
1995	Bill Cowher	11–5	1st/AFC champions
1996	Bill Cowher	10–6	1st/AFC Central champions
1997	Bill Cowher	11–5	1st/AFC Central co-champions
1998	Bill Cowher	7–9	3rd
1999	Bill Cowher	6–10	4th
2000	Bill Cowher	9–7	3rd
2001	Bill Cowher	13–3	1st/AFC Central champions
2002	Bill Cowher	10–5–1	1st/AFC North champions
2003	Bill Cowher	6–10	3rd
2004	Bill Cowher	15–1	1st/AFC North champions
2005	Bill Cowher	11–5	1st/Super Bowl champions
2006	Bill Cowher	8–8	2nd
2007	Mike Tomlin	10–6	1st/AFC North co-champions
2008	Mike Tomlin	12–4	1st/Super Bowl champions
2009	Mike Tomlin	9–7	2nd
Totals		529–495–20	

Note: The team was known as the Pittsburgh Pirates from 1933 through 1939. The 1943 team was called the Steagles (Steelers-Eagles), and the 1944 club was known as Card-Pitt (Cardinals-Pittsburgh).

Playoff Results

Date	Postseason Game	Result
12/21/47	NFL Eastern Division	Eagles 21, Steelers 0
1/6/63	NFL Playoff Bowl	Lions 17, Steelers 10
12/23/72	AFC divisional	Steelers 13, Raiders 7
12/31/72	AFC championship	Dolphins 21, Steelers 17
12/22/73	AFC divisional	Raiders 33, Steelers 14
12/22/74	AFC divisional	Steelers 32, Bills 14
12/29/74	AFC championship	Steelers 24, Raiders 13
1/12/75	Super Bowl IX	Steelers 16, Vikings 6
12/27/75	AFC divisional	Steelers 28, Colts 10
1/4/76	AFC championship	Steelers 16, Raiders 10
1/18/76	Super Bowl X	Steelers 21, Cowboys 17
12/19/76	AFC divisional	Steelers 40, Colts 14
12/26/76	AFC championship	Raiders 24, Steelers 7
12/24/77	AFC divisional	Broncos 34, Steelers 21
12/30/78	AFC divisional	Steelers 33, Broncos 10
1/7/79	AFC championship	Steelers 34, Oilers 5
1/21/79	Super Bowl XIII	Steelers 35, Cowboys 31
12/30/79	AFC divisional	Steelers 34, Dolphins 14
1/6/80	AFC championship	Steelers 27, Oilers 13
1/20/80	Super Bowl XIV	Steelers 31, Rams 19
1/9/83	AFC tournament	Chargers 31, Steelers 28
1/1/84	AFC divisional	Raiders 38, Steelers 10
12/30/84	AFC divisional	Steelers 24, Broncos 17
1/6/85	AFC championship	Dolphins 45, Steelers 28
12/31/89	AFC wild card	Steelers 26, Oilers 23
1/7/90	AFC divisional	Broncos 24, Steelers 23
1/9/93	AFC divisional	Bills 24, Steelers 3
1/8/94	AFC wild card	Chiefs 27, Steelers 24
1/7/95	AFC divisional	Steelers 29, Browns 9
1/15/95	AFC championship	Chargers 17, Steelers 13
1/6/96	AFC divisional	Steelers 40, Bills 21
1/14/96	AFC championship	Steelers 20, Colts 16
1/28/96	Super Bowl XXX	Cowboys 27, Steelers 17
12/29/96	AFC wild card	Steelers 42, Colts 14
1/5/97	AFC divisional	Patriots 28, Steelers 3
1/3/98	AFC divisional	Steelers 7, Patriots 6
1/11/98	AFC championship	Broncos 24, Steelers 21
1/20/02	AFC divisional	Steelers 27, Ravens 10

Date	Round	Result
1/27/02	AFC championship	Patriots 24, Steelers 17
1/5/03	AFC wild card	Steelers 36, Browns 33
1/11/03	AFC divisional	Titans 34, Steelers 31
1/15/05	AFC divisional	Steelers 20, Jets 17
1/23/05	AFC championship	Patriots 41, Steelers 27
1/8/06	AFC wild card	Steelers 31, Bengals 17
1/15/06	AFC divisional	Steelers 21, Colts 18
1/22/06	AFC championship	Steelers 34, Broncos 17
2/5/06	Super Bowl XL	Steelers 21, Seahawks 10
1/5/08	AFC wild card	Jaguars 31, Steelers 29
1/11/09	AFC divisional	Steelers 35, Chargers 24
1/18/09	AFC championship	Steelers 23, Ravens 14
2/1/09	Super Bowl XLIII	Steelers 27, Cardinals 23

Steelers Head Coaches

Coach	Seasons	Record
Forrest Douds	1933	3–6–2
Luby DiMelio	1934	2–10
Joe Bach	1935–36, 1952–53	21–27
John McNally	1937–39	6–19
Walt Kiesling	1939–44, 1954–56	30–55–5
Bert Bell	1941	0–2
Aldo Donelli	1941	0–5
Jim Leonard	1945	2–8
Jock Sutherland	1946–47	13–9–1
John Michelosen	1948–51	20–26–2
Buddy Parker	1957–64	51–47–6
Mike Nixon	1965	2–12
Bill Austin	1966–68	11–28–3
Chuck Noll	1969–91	193–148–1
Bill Cowher	1992–2006	149–90–1
Mike Tomlin	2007–09	31–17

Note: Records do not include playoff games.

Steelers with Most Pro Bowl Appearances

Player	Pro Bowls	Seasons
Joe Greene	10	1969–76, 1978–79
Ernie Stautner	9	1952–53, 1955–61
Franco Harris	9	1972–80
Jack Lambert	9	1975–83
Mike Webster	9	1978–85, 1987
Jack Ham	8	1973–80
Andy Russell	7	1968, 1970–75
Rod Woodson	7	1989–94, 1996
Dermontti Dawson	7	1992–98
Alan Faneca	7	2001–07
L. C. Greenwood	6	1973–76, 1978–79
Frank Varrichione	5	1955, 1957–58, 1960
Mel Blount	5	1975–76, 1978–79, 1980
Donnie Shell	5	1978–82
Greg Lloyd	5	1991–95
Troy Polamalu	5	2004–08
Casey Hampton	5	2003, 2005–07, 2009
Dale Dodrill	4	1953–55, 1957
Jack Butler	4	1955–58
Carnell Lake	4	1994–97
Jerome Bettis	4	1996–97, 2001, 2004
Hines Ward	4	2001–04

Steelers in the Pro Football Hall of Fame

Player	Position	Year
Bert Bell	Co-owner	1963
Mel Blount	CB	1989
Terry Bradshaw	QB	1989
Bill Dudley	RB	1966
Joe Greene	DT	1987
Jack Ham	LB	1988
Franco Harris	RB	1990
John Henry Johnson	RB	1987

STEELERS BY THE NUMBERS

Walt Kiesling	G/Coach	1966
Jack Lambert	LB	1990
Bobby Layne	QB	1967
John McNally	RB/Coach	1963
Chuck Noll	Coach	1993
Art Rooney	Founder	1964
Dan Rooney	Owner	2000
John Stallworth	WR	2002
Ernie Stautner	DT	1969
Lynn Swann	WR	2001
Mike Webster	C	1997
Rod Woodson	CB	2009

Other Hall of Famers with Steelers Experience

Len Dawson	QB	1987
Bill Hewitt	E	1971
Cal Hubbard	OT	1963
Marion Motley	RB	1968
Earle Neale	Coach	1969

Steelers Award Winners

1946	Bill Dudley—Joe F. Carr Trophy (NFL MVP)
1969	Joe Greene—NFL Defensive Rookie of the Year
1972	Chuck Noll—AFC Coach of the Year
	Franco Harris—NFL Offensive Rookie of the Year
	Joe Greene—NFL Defensive Player of the Year
1974	Jack Lambert—NFL Defensive Rookie of the Year
	Joe Greene—NFL Defensive Player of the Year
	Franco Harris—Super Bowl IX MVP
1975	Mel Blount—NFL Defensive Player of the Year
	Lynn Swann—Super Bowl X MVP
1976	Jack Lambert—NFL Defensive Player of the Year
1978	Terry Bradshaw—NFL MVP
	Terry Bradshaw—Super Bowl XIII MVP
1979	Jack Lambert—AFC Defensive Player of the Year
	Terry Bradshaw—Super Bowl XIV MVP
1984	Louis Lipps—NFL Offensive Rookie of the Year
	John Stallworth—NFL Comeback Player of the Year
1989	Chuck Noll—Maxwell Football Club NFL Coach of the Year
1992	Bill Cowher—*Sporting News*/AP NFL Coach of the Year
	Barry Foster—AFC Offensive Player of the Year
1993	Rod Woodson—NFL Defensive Player of the Year
1994	Greg Lloyd—AFC Defensive Player of the Year
1996	Jerome Bettis—NFL Comeback Player of the Year
2001	Kendrell Bell—NFL Defensive Rookie of the Year
2002	Tommy Maddox—NFL Comeback Player of the Year
2004	Bill Cowher—*Sporting News* NFL Coach of the Year
	Ben Roethlisberger—NFL Offensive Rookie of the Year
2005	Hines Ward—Super Bowl XL MVP
2008	James Harrison—NFL Defensive Player of the Year
	Santonio Holmes—Super Bowl XLIII MVP
	Mike Tomlin—NFL Coach of the Year

Steelers All-Time Leaders: Passing

	Name	Years	Attempts	Comp.	Yards	Pct.	TDs	Int.
1.	Terry Bradshaw	1970–83	3,901	2,025	27,989	51.9	212	210
2.	Ben Roethlisberger	2004–09	2,411	1,526	19,302	63.3	127	81
3.	Kordell Stewart	1995–2002	2,107	1,190	13,328	56.4	70	72
4.	Neil O'Donnell	1990–95	1,871	1,069	12,867	57.1	68	39
5.	Bubby Brister	1986–92	1,477	776	10,104	52.5	51	57
6.	Bobby Layne	1958–62	1,156	569	8,983	49.2	67	81
7.	Jim Finks	1949–55	1,382	661	8,854	47.8	55	88
8.	Mark Malone	1980–87	1,374	690	8,582	50.2	54	68
9.	Tommy Maddox	2001–2005	1,036	603	7,139	58.2	42	40
10.	Mike Tomczak	1993–99	973	546	6,649	56.1	37	43

PITTSBURGH STEELERS YESTERDAY & TODAY

Steelers All-Time Leaders: Rushing

Name	Years	Carries	Yards	Avg.	Long	TDs
1. Franco Harris	1972–83	2,881	11,950	4.1	75	91
2. Jerome Bettis	1996–2005	2,683	10,571	3.9	50	78
3. Willie Parker	2004–09	1,253	5,378	4.3	80	24
4. John Henry Johnson	1960–65	1,025	4,383	4.3	87	26
5. Frank Pollard	1980–88	953	3,989	4.2	56	20
6. Dick Hoak	1961–70	1,132	3,965	3.5	77	25
7. Barry Foster	1990–84	915	3,943	4.3	69	26
8. Rocky Bleier	1968, 1970–80	928	3,865	4.2	70	23
9. Walter Abercrombie	1982–87	842	3,343	4.0	50	22
10. Fran Rogel	1950–57	900	3,271	3.6	58	17

Steelers All-Time Leaders: Receiving

Name	Years	Total	Yards	Avg.	Long	TDs
1. Hines Ward	1998–2009	895	10,947	12.2	85	78
2. John Stallworth	1974–87	537	8,723	16.2	74	63
3. Louis Lipps	1984–91	358	6,018	16.8	89	39
4. Lynn Swann	1974–82	336	5,462	16.3	68	51
5. Elbie Nickel	1947–57	329	5,133	15.6	77	37
6. Buddy Dial	1959–63	219	4,723	21.6	88	42
7. Plaxico Burress	2000–04	261	4,164	16.0	62	22
8. Ray Mathews	1951–59	230	3,919	17.0	78	34
9. Santonio Holmes	2006–09	235	3,835	16.3	83	20
10. Roy Jefferson	1965–69	199	3,671	18.4	84	29

Steelers Single-Season Leaders: Passing

Passing Yards

Name	Yards	Season
1. Ben Roethlisberger	4,328	2009
2. Terry Bradshaw	3,724	1979
3. Ben Roethlisberger	3,513	2006
4. Tommy Maddox	3,414	2003
5. Terry Bradshaw	3,339	1980
6. Ben Roethlisberger	3,301	2008
7. Neil O'Donnell	3,208	1993
8. Ben Roethlisberger	3,154	2007
9. Kordell Stewart	3,109	2001
10. Kordell Stewart	3,020	1997

Touchdown Passes

Name	TDs	Season
1. Ben Roethlisberger	32	2007
2. Terry Bradshaw	28	1978
3. Terry Bradshaw	26	1979
3. Ben Roethlisberger	26	2009
5. Terry Bradshaw	24	1980
6. Terry Bradshaw	22	1981
7. Kordell Stewart	21	1997
7. Ed Brown	21	1963
9. 4 tied with 20		

Passer Rating

Name	Rating	Season
1. Ben Roethlisberger	104.1	2007
2. Ben Roethlisberger	100.5	2009
3. Ben Roethlisberger	98.6	2005
4. Ben Roethlisberger	98.1	2004
5. Terry Bradshaw	87.8	1975
6. Neil O'Donnell	87.7	1995
7. Tommy Maddox	85.2	2002
8. Terry Bradshaw	84.8	1978
9. Terry Bradshaw	84.0	1981
10. Neil O'Donnell	83.6	1992

Pass Attempts

Name	Attempts	Season
1. Tommy Maddox	519	2003
2. Ben Roethlisberger	506	2009
3. Neil O'Donnell	486	1993
4. Terry Bradshaw	472	1979
5. Ben Roethlisberger	469	2006
5. Ben Roethlisberger	469	2008

Pass Completions

Name	Completions	Season
1. Ben Roethlisberger	337	2009
2. Tommy Maddox	298	2003
3. Ben Roethlisberger	281	2008
4. Ben Roethlisberger	280	2006
5. Neil O'Donnell	270	1993

Steelers Single-Season Leaders: Rushing

Rushing Attempts

Name	Carries	Season
1. Barry Foster	390	1992
2. Jerome Bettis	375	1997
3. Jerome Bettis	355	2000
4. Willie Parker	337	2006
5. Willie Parker	321	2007

Rushing Yards

Name	Yards	Season
1. Barry Foster	1,690	1992
2. Jerome Bettis	1,665	1997
3. Willie Parker	1,494	2006
4. Jerome Bettis	1,431	1996
5. Jerome Bettis	1,341	2000
6. Willie Parker	1,316	2007
7. Franco Harris	1,246	1975
8. Willie Parker	1,202	2005
9. Franco Harris	1,186	1979
10. Jerome Bettis	1,185	1998

Rushing Touchdowns

Name	TDs	Season
1. Franco Harris	14	1976
2. Willie Parker	13	2006
2. Jerome Bettis	13	2004
4. Kordell Stewart	11	1997
4. Jerome Bettis	11	1996
4. Barry Foster	11	1992
4. Franco Harris	11	1979
4. Franco Harris	11	1977

Steelers Single-Season Leaders: Receiving

Receptions

Name	Receptions	Season
1. Hines Ward	112	2002
2. Hines Ward	95	2003
3. Hines Ward	95	2009
4. Hines Ward	94	2001
5. Yancey Thigpen	85	1995

Receiving Yards

Name	Yards	Season
1. Yancey Thigpen	1,398	1997
2. John Stallworth	1,395	1984
3. Hines Ward	1,329	2002
4. Plaxico Burress	1,325	2002
5. Yancey Thigpen	1,307	1995

Touchdown Receptions

Name	TDs	Season
1. Hines Ward	12	2002
1. Louis Lipps	12	1985
1. Buddy Dial	12	1961
4. Hines Ward	11	2005
4. John Stallworth	11	1984
4. Lynn Swann	11	1975
4. Lynn Swann	11	1978
4. Roy Jefferson	11	1968

Steelers All-Time Scoring Leaders

Name	Position	Points
1. Gary Anderson	PK	1,343
2. Jeff Reed	PK	855
3. Roy Gerela	PK	731
4. Franco Harris	RB	600
5. Hines Ward	WR	484

Steelers All-Time Sack Leaders

Name	Position	Sacks
1. Jason Gildon	LB	77.0
2. L. C. Greenwood	DE	73.5
3. Joe Greene	DT	66.0
4. Joey Porter	LB	60.0
5. Keith Willis	DE	59.0

Steelers All-Time Interception Leaders

Name	Position	Interceptions
1. Mel Blount	CB	57
2. Jack Butler	DB	52
3. Donnie Shell	SS	51
4. Rod Woodson	CB	38

Steelers Rushing Records

- Most rushing yards, game: 223, Willie Parker, 12/7/06 vs. Cleveland
- Most rushing touchdowns, game: 10 tied with 3; most recently, Willie Parker, 9/7/08 vs. Houston
- Highest rushing average, career: Kordell Stewart, 5.23
- Highest rushing average, season: Kordell Stewart, 5.8, 2001
- Longest run from scrimmage: 97 yards, Bobby Gage, 12/4/49 vs. Chicago Bears
- Most games with at least 100 yards, career: 50, Jerome Bettis
- Most games with at least 200 yards rushing, career: 2, Willie Parker

Steelers Passing Records

- Most completions, game: 38, Ben Roethlisberger, 11/5/06 vs. Denver
- Most passing yards, game: 503, Ben Roethlisberger, 12/20/09 vs. Green Bay
- Most passing touchdowns, game: 5, Terry Bradshaw, 11/15/81 vs. Atlanta; Mark Malone, 9/8/85 vs. Indianapolis; Ben Roethlisberger, 11/5/07 vs. Baltimore
- Longest completion: 90 yards, Terry Bradshaw to Mark Malone, 11/8/91 vs. Seattle; Bubby Brister to Dwight Stone, 10/14/90 vs. Denver; Kordell Stewart to Bobby Shaw, 12/16/01 vs. Baltimore

Steelers Receiving Records

- Most receptions, game: 14, Courtney Hawkins, 11/1/98 vs. Tennessee
- Most receiving yards, game: 253, Plaxico Burress, 11/10/02 vs. Atlanta
- Most touchdown receptions, game: 4, Roy Jefferson, 11/3/68 vs. Atlanta
- Most games with at least 100 yards receiving: 25, John Stallworth and Hines Ward

Steelers Miscellaneous Records

- Most kickoff return yards, career: 4,894, Rod Woodson
- Most kickoff return touchdowns, career: 3, Lynn Chandnois
- Most punt return yards, career: 2,362, Rod Woodson
- Most punt return touchdowns, career: 4, Antwaan Randle El
- Most field goals, career: 309, Gary Anderson
- Highest punting average, career: 45.7, Bobby Joe Green

INDEX

A
African Americans, 27
American Bowl, 94
American Football Conference (AFC), 36
American Football League (AFL), 36
Anderson, Gary, 77
Anderson, Larry, 63
Austin, Bill, 28

B
Bach, Joe, 18, 30
Bahr, Matt, 66, 67
Baltimore Ravens, 101
Batch, Charlie, 120
Bell, Bert, 15, 16
Bell, Kendrell, 131
Bell, Myron, 88, 110
Bell, Theo, 62
Berlin, Ralph, 37, 74, 75
Berman, Morris, 19
Bettis, Jerome "The Bus," 61, 95, 99, 105, 110, 117, 118, 119
black and gold, 29
Black Menace, 60
Bleier, Rocky, 33, 48, 52, 53, 59, 62, 63, 64, 65, 66, 73
Blitzburgh, 83, 102
Blount, Mel, 31, 40, 45, 57, 63, 64, 72
blown calls, 99
Bradshaw, Terry
  biography, 38–39
  on Chuck Noll, 35
  Immaculate Reception, 40–41
  injuries, 39, 53, 73
  memorabilia, 71, 78
  and Oakland Raiders, 60
  returns to Pittsburgh, 109
  1970 draft, 40
  1974 season (Super Bowl IX), 35, 42, 43, 44, 45
  1975 season (Super Bowl X), 39, 52, 53, 55
  1976, 62
  1978 season (Super Bowl XIII), 33, 39, 62, 64, 65
  1979 season (Super Bowl XIV), 66, 67, 68
Brady, Pat, 26
Brandt, Jim, 21
Brister, Bubby, 75, 76, 85
Brown, Chad, 88
Brown, Larry, 40, 77
Bruener, Mark, 88
Buckner, Brentson, 88
Burrell, John, 25
Burress, Plaxico, 101, 111
Butler, Jack, 18, 24, 26–27, 51, 89

C
Card-Pitt, 16
Carpenter, Preston, 25
Carr, Joe, 19
Carson, Bud, 56, 72
Chandnois, Lynn, 19, 24, 26
cheerleaders, 28
Cherundolo, Chuck, 15
Chiodo, Joe, 19, 23
Cincinnati Bengals, 98
Cleveland Browns, 73, 101
Colclough, Ricardo, 118
Collier, Mike, 53
Colon, Willie, 132
Cope, Myron, 87, 96, 105, 112, 121
Cowher, Bill
  on Ben Roethlisberger, 113, 116
  biography, 82–83
  on Hines Ward, 112
  on Jerome Bettis, 95
  memorabilia, 93
  on 1990s Steelers, 103
  1992 season, 80, 84
  1995 season (Super Bowl XXX), 91
  2001 season, 110
  2005 season (Super Bowl XL), 116, 117, 118, 119
  2006 season, 120
Craft, Russ, 21
Cuff, Ward, 15
Cunningham, Bennie, 62, 66, 67

D
Davis, Carey, 123
Davis, Steve, 40
Dawson, Dermontti, 84, 88, 91, 102
Deloplaine, Jack "The Hydroplane," 63
Depression era, 13, 14
Dial, Buddy, 25, 26
Dodrill, Dale, 21, 26
Dole, Robin, 77
Donahoe, Tom, 50, 75, 82, 84, 94, 96
Donelli, Buff, 15
Dudley, Bill "Bluefield Bullet," 17

F
face guards, 21
Faneca, Alan, 118, 119, 131
fans, 23, 61, 65, 92, 96–97
Farrior, James, 118, 123, 130
Finks, Jim, 18, 19, 20, 21, 30
Forbes Field, 12, 19
Foster, Barry, 84
Fuamatu-Ma'afala, Chris, 111
Fuqua, John "Frenchy," 41, 53
Furness, Steve, 52

G
Gaona, Bob, 21
Gerela, Roy, 53, 55, 62, 64
Gildon, Jason, 103, 105
Gilliam, Joe "Jefferson Street," 38, 42, 43
Greene, Joe "Mean Joe"
  biography, 37
  Coke commercial, 78
  on Franco Harris, 48
  injuries, 53
  memorabilia, 78
  on Oakland Raiders, 60
  Steel Curtain, 56–57
  1969 draft, 40
  1974 season (Super Bowl IX), 44, 45
  1975 season (Super Bowl X), 54
  1979 season (Super Bowl XIV), 68
Greene, Kevin, 88, 93, 103
Greenwood, L. C., 40, 44, 45, 52, 53, 54, 55, 56–57
Grigas, Johnny, 19
Grossman, Randy, 67

H
Ham, Jack, 35, 40, 45, 49, 57, 59, 74, 93
Hampton, Casey, 117, 131, 132
Hanratty, Terry, 38, 42
Harris, Franco
  biography, 48
  fans, 61, 79
  Immaculate Reception, 40–41
  memorabilia, 46, 70, 78
  1972 draft, 40
  1974 season, 43
  1974 season (Super Bowl IX), 44, 45
  1975 season (Super Bowl X), 52, 53
  1976, 62
  1976 season, 73
  1978 season (Super Bowl XIII), 62, 65
  1979 season (Super Bowl XIV), 66, 67, 68
Harrison, James, 123, 126, 127, 128, 130, 132, 135
Harrison, Reggie, 55
Hart, Jack, 29
Hartings, Jeff, 131
Hartwig, Justin, 128
Hastings, Andre, 84, 88
Heinz Company, 114
Heinz Field, 108–9, 115
helmets, 10, 25, 29
Henry, Mike, 31
Hinkle, Bryan, 77
Hoak, Dick, 25, 27, 30, 34, 38, 49, 56, 109
Hoge, Merril, 75
Hoke, Chris, 120
Holmes, Ernie "Fats," 37, 40, 56–57
Holmes, Santonio, 126, 127, 128, 129, 131, 132, 134
Hood, Ziggy, 132

I
Ilkin, Tunch, 39, 76, 77, 89, 100
Immaculate Interception, 128, 135
Immaculate Reception, 40–41
Immaculate Redemption, 117, 118, 124
Iron City brewery, 30, 46

J
Jackson, Earnest, 77
Jackson, John, 85
jerseys, 29, 58
Johnson, Charles, 84
Johnson, John Henry, 25, 26
Johnson, Norm, 88, 89, 90, 91

K
Kalis, Todd, 85
Keisel, Brett, 129
Kemp, Ray, 27
Kiesling, Walt, 18, 20
Kirkland, Levon, 88, 89, 90, 103
Kolb, Jon, 40
Kruczek, Mike, 73

L
Lake, Carnell, 82, 84, 88, 89, 90, 91, 94, 103
Lambert, Jack
  biography, 49
  and Browns, 73
  fan club, 59

143

memorabilia, 59, 93
1974 draft, 42
1974 season (Super Bowl IX), 44
1975 season (Super Bowl X), 52, 53, 54, 55
1979 season (Super Bowl XIV), 68, 69
Layne, Bobby, 24–25, 31
Lewis, Frank, 40
Lipps, Louis, 76, 77
Lipscomb, Eugene "Big Daddy," 26
Little, David, 77
Lloyd, Greg, 75, 84, 88, 90, 93, 103

M
Maddox, Tommy, 111, 113, 115, 116, 117
Malone, Mark, 74
Mansfield, Ray, 27, 28, 30, 34
mascot, Steely McBeam, 114
McNally, John "Johnny Blood," 14–15
memorabilia, 20–21, 30–31, 46–47, 58–59, 70–71, 78–79, 92–93, 104–5, 114–15, 124–25, 134–35
Mendenhall, Rashard, 101, 132
Merriweather, Mike, 74, 77
Michelosen, John, 18, 21
Miller, Heath, 124, 127
Mills, Ernie, 84, 88, 89, 90
Moore, Mewelde, 126
Morris, Bam, 81, 88, 89, 90
Mosley, Matt, 96–97

N
National Football League (NFL), 12, 36
Nickel, Elbie, 18, 21, 26
Nixon, Mike, 28
Noll, Chuck
 on Ben Roethlisberger, 113
 biography, 34–35
 on drafting players, 74
 on the Immaculate Reception, 41
 on Kordell Stewart, 110
 memorabilia, 46
 and Oakland Raiders, 60
 retirement, 75
 on Three Rivers Stadium, 61
 1969 season, 32
 on 1969–72 drafts, 40, 42
 1974 draft, 42
 1975 season (Super Bowl X), 55
 1978 season (Super Bowl XIII), 62, 63, 65
 1979 season (Super Bowl XIV), 68
Nunn, Bill, 27, 35

O
Oakland Raiders, 60
O'Donnell, Neil, 82, 84, 85, 88, 89, 90, 91, 92, 93, 99
Oldham, Chris, 90
Olsavsky, Jerry, 88, 90
one for the thumb, 74

P
Parker, Buddy, 24, 25, 26–27, 28, 126
Parker, Willie, 107, 116, 117, 118, 119, 120, 123, 126, 127, 130
Pearson, Preston, 36
Pegram, Erric, 89
Perles, George, 56, 68–69
Perry, Darren, 88
Perry, Lowell, 27
Peterson, Ted, 66
Phillips, Bum, 66
Phil-Pitt Eagles, 16
Pittsburgh, 22–23
Pittsburgh Majestics, 11
Pittsburgh Maulers, 74
Pittsburgh Pirates, 12, 13, 20
Pitt Stadium, 19
players strike, 42
Playoff Bowl, 25
Polamalu, Troy, 114, 116, 117, 121, 123, 128, 130, 132, 135
Pollard, Frank, 74
Porter, Joey, 115, 117, 118, 124, 130

R
Randle El, Antwaan, 114, 117, 118, 119, 122
Reed, Jeff, 113, 116, 117, 123, 126, 127, 128
Roethlisberger, Ben "Big Ben"
 biography, 101, 113
 Immaculate Redemption, 117, 124
 memorabilia, 124, 135
 on the Terrible Towel, 121
 2004 season, 113
 2005 season (Super Bowl XL), 116, 117, 118, 119
 2006 season, 120
 2007 season, 123
 2008 season (Super Bowl XLIII), 126, 127, 129
 2009 season, 132, 133
Rogel, Fran, 26
Rooney, Art, (the Chief), 12–13, 15, 16, 45, 75, 115
Rooney, Art, Jr.
 on Ben Roethlisberger, 113
 on Depression-era football, 14
 and Heinz Field, 108
 on his father, 10, 12, 75
 on Kordell Stewart, 100
 on Mike Tomlin, 122
 and ownership shake-up, 122
 on Tommy Maddox, 111
 on 1974 draft, 42
Rooney, Dan
 and AFL, 36
 on Bill Austin, 28
 on Bill Cowher, 82–83, 120
 on Bill Dudley, 17
 biography, 50
 on Bobby Lane, 24
 on Buddy Parker, 24
 and Chuck Noll, 34
 on Franco Harris, 48
 on Heinz Field, 108
 on his father's way with people, 12–13
 on lack of depth in 1950s, 18
 on Mean Joe Greene, 37
 on Myron Cope, 87
 and ownership shake-up, 122
 on Steel Curtain, 56
 on Steelers' success, 68
 on Steelmark symbol, 29
 Super Bowl XL, 119
 on Terry Bradshaw, 38
 on three-way sale-swap, 15
 on 1992 receivers, 84
Rozelle, Pete, 36, 45
rule changes, 99
Russell, Andy, 27, 28, 34, 37, 43, 49, 52, 53, 54, 57, 93
Russell, Gary, 127, 128

S
Schweder, Jon, 21
Seals, Ray, 88
Searcy, Leon, 84, 85
Shell, Donnie, 57, 72
Smith, Aaron, 131
Smith, Jim, 66
Smith, W. Eugene, 22–23
Stallworth, John, 42, 51, 54, 62, 63, 64, 65, 66, 67, 68, 69
Stapleton, Darnell, 129
Stautner, Ernie, 18, 25, 26, 31, 78
Steagles, 16, 20
Steed, Joel, 88
Steel Curtain, 43, 44, 56–57, 58
Steelerettes, 28
steel industry, 22–23
Steelmark symbol, 29
Stewart, Kordell "Slash," 88, 89, 90, 94, 100, 104, 105, 110
Strzelczyk Justin "Jugs," 85
Super Bowl IX, 42, 43, 44, 45, 46, 47, 48
Super Bowl X, 52, 54, 55, 58, 59
Super Bowl XIII, 33, 51, 64–65
Super Bowl XXX, 81, 85, 88, 90–91, 92
Super Bowl XL, 112, 118, 119, 125
Super Bowl XLIII, 97, 128–29, 134, 135
Sutherland, Jock, 16
Swann, Lynn, 42, 45, 51, 52, 53, 54–55, 60, 62, 63, 64, 65, 121

T
tailgating, 61
Taylor, Ike, 119
Terrible Towel, 97, 98, 121
Thigpen, Yancey, 84, 88, 89, 90, 91, 102–3
Thomas, Clendon, 28
Thomas, J. T., 44, 54, 57, 66
Thompson, Alexis "Lex," 15
Thompson, Weegie, 74
Thornton, Sidney, 62, 66
Three Rivers Stadium, 61
Tittle, Y. A., 19
Tomczak, Mike, 94
Tomlin, Mike, 97, 106, 122, 123, 126, 129, 131, 133
Townsend, Deshea, 111, 127
Tucker, Ross, 97
Tuman, Jerame, 110
Turnpike Rivalry, 73

U
Unitas, Johnny, 18
United States Football League (USFL), 74
University of Pittsburgh, 19, 108

V
Varrichione, Frank, 26

W
Wagner, Mike, 35, 40, 53, 55, 57
Wallace, Mike, 133
Ward, Hines
 biography, 112
 on Kordell Stewart, 110
 memorabilia, 135
 on Ravens rivalry, 101
 2002 season, 111
 2005 season (Super Bowl XL), 117, 119, 125
 2007 season, 123
 2008 season (Super Bowl XLIII), 126
 2009 season, 132, 133
Washington, Nate, 127
Webster, Mike "Iron Mike," 42, 53, 65, 76
White, Byron "Whizzer," 13, 14
White, Dwight "Mad Dog," 40, 43, 44, 45, 53, 54, 56–57, 67
Williams, John, 89
Williams, Willie, 88
Winston, Dennis "Dirt," 66
Woodley, LaMarr, 126, 129, 132–33
Woodruff, Dwayne, 77
Woodson, Rod, 75, 82–83, 84, 86, 93, 94, 104
World War II era, 15, 16, 20

Z
Zereoue, Amos, 110